Sent **He** **Forth**
HIS WORD

He Sent Forth His Word

Series 5: Homilies for Feasts and Solemnities

Fr. Emmanuel Okami

EDITORS

Lisa Timms
Francis Sebastian Ofomata
Karen Littleton

IMPRIMATUR
Bishop Ayo Maria Atoyebi, OP
Bishop Emeritus of Ilorin Diocese, Nigeria

NIHIL OBSTAT
Very Rev. Fr. Stephen Audu
Ilorin Diocese,
Resident at St. Peter and All Hallow's Catholic Church,
Sacramento, California, US.
Former Rector, Seminary of St. Peter the Apostle,
Eruku, Kwara State, Nigeria

COVER ART
Senux Media
www.senuxmedia.com

EDITORS
Lisa Timms
Customer Manager, Global Operations, British Airways Plc.
Our Lady of Peace Parish, Burnham, UK.

Francis Sebastian Ofomata
Seminarian, Benin Archdiocese

Karen Littleton
Executive Coach and Mentor
Parishioner of St. Thomas Aquinas and
All Saints Parish, Bletchley, UK.

First Published 2020

ISBN 979-865-105-309-4

Published by
Communications Centre
Catholic Diocese of Ilorin Printing Press
Beside M&M Pastoral & Events Centre,
G.R.A, Offa Road,
Ilorin, Kwara State, Nigeria.

DEDICATION

I dedicate this book to

the parishioners of

Christ the King Parish, Bacita, Nigeria

St Michael's Parish, Isolo-Opin, Nigeria.

The Catholic Church of the Presentation,
Ikeja, GRA, Lagos, Nigeria

FOREWORD

Joy for the heart and light for the eyes.

It was with much joy and gladness that I accepted the invitation from the author, Rev. Fr. Emmanuel Okami, to write the foreword to two of his publications; Homilies for the Liturgical Seasons and Homilies for Feasts and Solemnities. Having known Fr. Okami for quite a while, I did not hesitate to concede to his request. These publications are evidently fruits of intense prayer, indepth study and inestimable pastoral engagements, which are now being codified for the edification of a wider audience and further divulgation of the Eternal Word.

The word, the heavens and the earth were made by the Word. God spoke and it came to be. Man was made by means of the Word. In Genesis 1: 26, with the use of the divine plural, a celestial invitation Let us, metamorphosed into the creation of the only being on earth who was made in the image and likeness of an eternal being. The immediacy in the manifestation of the Word showed the power in the enunciation. Post hoc, propter hocthe effect was seen as soon as the Word was pronounced. All that was made by the Word was good and man was the crown of God's creation: after the creation of man, *God saw all that he had made, and indeed, it was very good* (cf. Genesis 1:31).

It is no wonder then that when man fell from grace, God deemed it not a waste, in the fullness of time, to

v

send His only begotten Son, the Logos, to redeem man from sin and death. The world that was created by the Word can only be saved by the Word. This Word came to live and die among us, a man like us in all things but sin. Even after returning to the Father, the Word continues to live among us as He promised: I will be with you, until the end of time (Matthew 28:20). The Church, the body of the Word, is sanctified by the Word: *Y ou have already been cleansed by the word that I have spoken to you* (John 15:3).

In the Church, every Priest is chosen by God from among men and put in charge of things pertaining to God; to offer gifts and sacrifices for sins (Hebrews 5:1). The Priest is a minister of God and a messenger of God's Word. The Priest is very much like apocalyptic John who in Revelations 10:10 takes the open scroll from the angel and eats it. It was sweet as honey in the mouth but bitter in the stomach. The bitterness stands for the justice which the Word of God evokes, because the Word of God is sharper than any double-edged sword piercing even to dividing soul and spirit (cf. Hebrews 4:16). The Word is sweet in the mouth because it is like the river that gives life everywhere it flows. It is a healing balm which soothes the wounds of the soul and brings life, not death, to its hearer.

Every Priest has the onus to preach the word of God in season and out of season (cf. 2 Timothy 4:2). Canon 762 states, *The people   of God are first united through the word of the living God and are fully entitled to seek this word from their Priests. For this reason, sacred ministers are to consider the office of preaching as of great importance, since proclaiming the Gospel of God to all is among their principal duties.* Fr. Okami has definitely taken the office of preaching with great seriousness and his succinct explanation of the Word of Life has endeared many to Christ and made many once again interested in the Church.

Far from being abstract and difficult to understand, these reflections are consistently straight to the point and very much connected with daily life. The pages are spiced with stories which stem from real life experiences and with anecdotes that are capable of jolting any reader to spiritual consciousness. The author often gives his points in bullet style which makes comprehension and application quite easy. He also caps his reflections with practical hints for the reader, such that there is no ambiguity on the demands of the Word. Furthermore, the reflections on Sundays systematically explain each of the readings, including the Responsorial Psalm. It does not focus only on the Gospel, as seen in some other reflection booklets. This is a commendable approach and emphasises once more, the attention that the author pays to every Word of God read during the sacred liturgy.

It is very providential that Fr. Okami is publishing these meditations on the Word of God in year 2020, when the Church marks the 1600th anniversary of the death of Saint Jerome, the patron saint for biblical scholars. This same year is the tenth anniversary of the release of highly profound and rich Post-Synodal Apostolic Exhortation, Verbum Domini, a document which explores the importance of the Word of God in the

Church and its proclamation to the world in contemporary times. Fr. Okami's publication again has a special nexus with his current fidei donum location, the diocese of Northampton, as the Catholic Bishops of England and Wales have declared year 2020 as the Year of the Word. Without mincing words, there is no better time and clime for these publications by Fr. Okami.

I encourage all to get these reflections for themselves and their loved ones. These pearls of prayer and wisdom are veritable guides in the search for a deeper understanding of the Word of God and in the journey towards Christian perfection. Scour and devour these pages and let them be joy for your heart and light for your path.

Rev. Fr. Francis Adelabu, PhD
Saints Peter and Paul Major Seminary,
Bodija, Ibadan,Nigeria.

AUTHOR'S NOTE

I am immensely grateful to God for the grace to realise this onerous project. I received the inspiration to start this project back in 2016, however it has pleased God in His wise providence that this work be completed this significant year.

This year the Church marks the 1600th anniversary of the death of St Jerome, the Patron Saint for biblical scholars. This year is also the tenth anniversary of the release of the rich and spectacular Post Synodal Apostolic Exhortation, *Verbum Domini,* a document on the importance and relevance of the Word of God in our modern world.

So, it is God's phenomenal plan that this humble work, which began four years ago, be completed at this time.

He Sent Forth His Voice is a seven series books of homilies for Sundays (Year A, B, C), Weekdays (Cycle I and II), Liturgical seasons (Advent, Christmas, Lent and Easter), Feasts and Solemnities.

I want the reader to take note that some of the homilies were written and delivered in Africa (Nigeria), and some were written and delivered in Europe (England) and so this dynamism comes to play when reading these reflections. I have also tried to intentionally re-work some of the homilies to have a more universal countenance. However, no matter the original context and diverse cultural experiences, the Word of God still speaks to everyone in various ways.

I do not presume that everyone will agree with all the contents of these reflections; not even the Holy Bible can claim such a universal acceptance. However, what I pray and hope for is that these homilies will be of benefit to someone seeking to understand the Word of God and grow in faith. I also pray that this humble work may help preachers and teachers of the faith in their ministry of teaching.

My special thanks to all the Bishops who reviewed these books and offered vital and helpful suggestions. I am indebted to all those who edited these works; they have passed across the table of many editors but that is not to claim that they are flawless. My aim is not to write a flawless book, but to share with others the fruits of my meditation and the riches of God's Holy Word.

Many thanks to all who supported these publications in one way or the other. If God wills, this will be the beginning of many more to come.

May the revelation of the Word of God bring us light and understanding and lead us to Jesus who is the Word made Flesh, the Truth, The Way and the Life.

Father Emmanuel Okami
A Priest of Ilorin Diocese, Nigeria,
On Mission in Northampton Diocese, UK.
Word of Life Ministry (WOLM), Milton Keynes, UK,

REVIEWS

The sterling beauty of the Word of God cannot but be cherished, especially when it is given a unique touch through a simple but profound explication, which makes it really a double-edged sword, that wounds but ultimately leads to a fulfilled life. This is exactly what marks out this beautiful book of reflection as distinctive. Embellished also with the Magisterium and lives of the Saints, Fr. Emmanuel demonstrates himself a scriptural adept by giving the entire reflection the needed synthesis and dynamism that facilitate faith's voyage. Enjoy!

Fr. Stanley Orazulike
Faculty of Theology of Lugano, Switzerland

Fr. Okami has beautifully put these reflections together to nourish us. They are so practical and down to earth, and can be used by individuals, families and for group reflections. The best way to reflect on these reflections is to use them for prayer - lectio divina, which involves prayerfully and slowly reading the texts before reading the reflections, then praying with them and asking God to reposition us and purify our desires and intentions to be ready for his coming into our hearts in the experiences of life.

Fr Luke Dominic Onwe, OCD
Prior and Students' Director
Discalced Carmelite Formation House,
Ibadan, Nigeria.

This book presents a comprehensive coverage of the Catholic Feasts and Solemnities, from the most popular ones to those that are more obscure, but equally important. For each Feast or Solemnity, the author presents the relevant scripture reading; an analysis of its historical and religious context; and perhaps, most importantly, what the reader can take from it, in the form of clear and concise personal actions.

The author's style is simple, clear and warm, not shying away from directly reminding the reader to examine their personal daily lives in the light of these readings. The reader's experience after absorbing this book is a much clearer and informed knowledge of some of the deeper mysteries of the Catholic Feasts and Solemnities, and how these relate them on an individual basis.

Dr Anthony Kakhu
Our Lady of Peace Catholic Parish, Burnham, UK.

I've always known Rev Father Emmanuel Okami to be of many talents. This book comes as no surprise. The simplicity of his ideas attracts followers as moths are attracted to a flame. With an aim that is true and sure, Father Okamibrings the Word of God very near to us all, in the reflections contained in this book. It is a MUST READ.

Oselumhense Anetor
Pastor at St Patrick Catholic Church, Urohi,
Catholic Diocese of Uromi, Edo State, Nigeria
Director of Fada Kay's World @ fadakay.org

In this compilation of work, Father Emmanuel Okami makes Holy Scriptures accessible to all by sharing his interpretation of Mass readings. In his wisdom, Father Okami shares daily reflections that guide the reader to live a Christian life. This is an inspired work which reflects the central importance of the Holy Scriptures. I would recommend this book to anyone who wants to experience a true encounter with Jesus Christ.

Marjorie Le Gall, MA.
St Thomas Aquinas and All Saints Parish,
Bletchley, UK.

TABLE OF CONTENTS

Mary Mother of God
Solemnity
———❧❧❧———

READING TEXTS: *Numbers 6:22-27; Psalm 66:2-8; Galatians 4:4-7; Luke 2:16-21.*

The role of Mary in our salvation

Today the Holy Mother Church celebrates the Divine Motherhood of our Blessed Virgin Mary.

This day is also significant because it is the first day of a new calendar year. The Church also celebrates it as a world day of peace.

It is appropriate that we begin this New Year by reflecting on the excellence of our Blessed Mother and by asking for her maternal solace, patronage and charity.

Being the mother of the Prince of Peace, the Church also honours Mary as the Queen of Peace and so we pray especially, through her intercession, for peace in the world during this New Year and in our lives.

The Catholic Church is often criticised for her devotion to Mary. Critics have claimed that the Church makes Mary equal to Jesus and that Mary is 'worshipped'. Some of these critics have also said: She is not important, she is just a vessel.

Let me state here that there are four things that the devil hates:

I.   A united family.
II. A united church.
III. Holiness in a person, especially a priest.

1

IV. Devotion to the Blessed Mother.

With respect to IV, Pope Francis says: *wher e Mary is, the devil does not enter.* (Pope Francis, Mass at Basilica of St. Mary Major, Rome, January 28, 2018).

The Italian priest Santé Babolin (who also taught at the Gregorian University in Rome). said that Satan is behind the attacks, in various parts of the world, against the Virgin Mary: *in   the face of the failure of the onslaught by non-believers, now, in order to offend and confound the Catholic people, the Virgin Mary, whom the devil hates, is being attacked.*

Father Babolin also notes that Mary is a powerful advocate for him during exorcisms: *In   my experience, so far I have performed 2,300 rites of exorcism, I can say that the invocation of the Most Holy Virgin Mary often provokes significant reactions in the person being exorcized*   (in Desde la Fe, March 8, 2018, 3.25pm).

Because of the role of the Blessed Virgin Mary, as the Mother of the Holy Son of God who will save us from our sin, God preserved her from all stain of sin from the first instant of her conception. She was given a unique holiness so as to be well-equipped for her role in the salvation of humanity.

God's plan was materialised in her when she consented to be the mother of the Saviour. God did not force divine maternity on her.   He sought her assent when the Angel Gabriel was sent to her.

Even though Mary was not sure of the implications for her, she gave her consent. In Luke 1:38 she declared: *Behold, I am the handmaid of the Lord, let it be done to me according to your word.*   At that instant, the Son of God took flesh in her and she became the Mother of God the Son.

Since she gave her assent wholeheartedly to God's plan for redeeming humanity, she is also instrumental in bringing about salvation for the whole world. She plays a secondary role in the redemption of humanity.

Her Yes was not just instantaneous, but continuous, even until the Cross. She was actively engaged as if nailed completely with Jesus. It is as a result of her suffering with her Son that the Church calls her Queen of Martyrs. In being a spiritual martyr, at the foot of the Cross, she contributes to our salvation.

This is why she is often invoked under the titles: Co-redemptrix, Mediatrix of All Graces, Mother of the Church and Advocate.

In a vision the Blessed Virgin Mother revealed to St. Bridget, *ther e is no sinner in the world, however much she may be at enmity with God, who does not return to Him and recover His grace* , if she has recourse to her and asks for her assistance.

The Church says in the Document of Vatican II on the Church*: This Motherhood of Mary in the order of grace continues uninterruptedly from the consent which she loyally gave at the Annunciation and which she sustained without wavering beneath the Cross, until the eternal fulfilment of all the elect. Taken up to heaven, she did not lay aside this saving office but by her manifold intercession, continues to bring us the gifts of salvation. By her maternal charity, she cares for the brethren of her son, who still journey on earth surrounded by dangers and difficulties until they are led into their blessed home.* (CCC 969, LG 62).

Mary's life is an example to us. It is a constant reminder that we must all work alongside the Redeemer in bringing the saving Gospel of Christ into the world.

We are to offer our meritorious sufferings for the glory of God and the salvation of souls in the order of the priesthood of the laity. Also, in the ministerial priesthood, we are to participate, through acts of charity and Christian works of mercy, in the application of the graces of Calvary to the world today.

Learning from the School of Mary

We learn these four lessons from our Blessed Mother:

I. We are created for a purpose (Ephesians 1:4; 2:10).
II. We should be patient in suffering. She endured her sorrows with patience and faith.
III. Obedience and total surrender to God in all things.
IV. The virtues of chastity, humility and charity.

We pray that, through her intercession, we may learn to say Y es to the Lord daily and, that we may learn to bear our crosses this year with faith, courage and patience. May she, who is the Queen of Peace, intercede for the whole world that we may enjoy the peace that only God gives.

The Epiphany of the Lord
Solemnity

A REFLECTION ON HERODIC SPIRIT

READING TEXTS: *Isaiah 60:1-6; Psalm 72; Ephesians 3:2-3, 5-6; Matthew 2:1-12*

On the 25th of December, we celebrated the Birth of Christ; today, we celebrate the fact that Jesus was born into a family. This affords us an opportunity to reflect on the importance of the family.

Today is the feast of the Epiphany. On this feast, there is so much to reflect on. Whilst I shall consider the different reactions to the Good News about Jesus, my specific focus will be on the reactions of Herod.
There are three principal characters in today's Gospel: The wise men, the chief priests and Scribes and Herod.

I.   The wise men
According to many commentators, these wise men are also astrologers, priests, philosophers and kings from the East. They have been identified, in tradition, as Melchior, Balthasar and Caspar. These wise men followed the star to look for Jesus; they stopped at nothing to find Him. They were never discouraged by the indifference of the Jews, who were supposed to be excited about the news. When the wise men saw Jesus, they worshipped Him and gave Him three significant gifts.

They were indeed wise men, because only wise people look for Jesus, worship Him and offer Him their best. They represent a positive response to Jesus.

5

II. The chief priests and scribes

Herod immediately consulted the chief priests and scribes about the message of the Magi, and they were quick to give an answer quoting Micah 5:2. Sadly, they were too indifferent to take heed of the event, even though they were just six miles away from Jerusalem. They knew the scripture, but it did them no good

This is another reaction to Jesus - indifference. Many people are simply indifferent to Jesus; they aren't concerned about Him.

This spirit of the scribes is in our midst today; many people are just uninterested in what we say or believe about Jesus; they may ask us to pray for me, but they are not too bothered about drawing close to God.

Interestingly, this spirit is also prevalent in some who come to Church. There are people who attend Church but are indifferent to the Gospel message. They are not prepared to make any commitment; they know what the church teaches, but what difference does it make? Their faith does not affect how they live.

III. Herod

I will now pay specific attention to Herod. Thankfully, through the work of Josephus the historian, we have access to lots of interesting details concerning Herod and his response.

Herod became a governor of Galilee in 47BC when he was just 25 years old. In 40BC, the Roman Senate proclaimed that he was the king of the Jews because he was able to maintain peace and stability, although via cruel means. The Jews hated the fact that this title had been bestowed upon Herod, because he was not a Jew by birth or religion.

Herod was a paranoid tyrant, who used power to protect power. He was cruel, clever, envious, always suspicious and insecure. He could not tolerate those rivalling his power. For Herod, saving his throne was more important than saving his soul.

Herod killed his wife Mariamne, and three of his sons, on suspicion of treason. He also killed his mother-in-law, drowned a high priest and killed several of his uncles and cousins.

Now (at a very old age, after ruling for 41 years) he heard from the Magi, from the East, that a king had been born and he felt threatened. The old demon in him came alive again; he became insanely jealous and with no time to rest, he ordered the killing of all the male infants in Bethlehem, aged two years and under.

Herod died about 2,000 years ago but his spirit lives on. His descendants are still with us today. His spirit lives on in anyone who sees Jesus Christ as a threat and hates to hear anything about Him or about His Church. These descendants of Herod are those St. John called the anti-Christ (1 John 2:18-19).

Every misuse of power, every act of cruelty, violence and wickedness against the innocent, especially against children, is Herodic in spirit.

Finally, the tendency in people to see life as a competition, to be envious, to be suspicious, to feel threatened by others or to experience unwarranted feelings of insecurity is Herodic in spirit. Such Herodic tendencies kill relationships. When we begin to see others as posing a threat to our relevance, when the success and excellence of others evokes envy, when we become unnecessarily suspicious of people, seeing them as rivals, we are exhibiting something of Herod. These tendencies destroy our inner peace, rob us of our integrity and contradict completely our identity as children of God, created in His image and likeness.

The Baptism of the Lord
Feast

READING TEXTS: *Isaiah 42:1-4, 6-7; Psalm 29; Acts 10:34-38; Matthew 3:13-17*

Today, the Holy Mother Church celebrates the feast of the Baptism of the Lord. This celebration marks the end of the Christmas season.

Today, there are so many things we can reflect on. We can reflect on our own baptismal promises and how well we are fulfilling them. I thought of sharing some thoughts on God, parenthood and obligations; explaining the mystery of baptism drawing insights from the baptism of Jesus.

However, today, I have chosen to preach on the significance of the baptism of Jesus and a lesson to learn from John's reluctance.

For six months, John had been preaching repentance and the confession of sin. He baptised people as a sign of their repentance and resolution to be part of the kingdom of the Messiah. John has said so many awesome things about the Messiah; he has testified so much to His power, divinity, righteousness and grace. People were already very eager and desperately expectant.

After all John's publicity about Jesus, John beheld Him coming from Galilee to Jordan. Jesus came in simplicity, queuing up with other sinners; He also wanted to be baptised.

John was embarrassed. How was he to explain to people that this was the Messiah and that He also needed baptism? This did not make sense to John and John knew it would not make sense to people. No wonder, we are told, that John kept trying to dissuade Him (diekoluen). How can a prophet baptise God the Son? How can one who is sent to speak God's word, baptise God's word? How can a messenger baptise the sender? How can the one who is sinless, and has come to take away sins, be baptised by a sinner for the forgiveness of sin?

However, Jesus insisted. He told John: *leave   it like this for the time being; it is fitting that we should, in this way, do all that righteousness demands.* Then John agreed, not because he understood, there was no way he could understand. He agreed because Jesus insisted on it. John simply trusted and obeyed.

I remember an incident that occurred shortly after I had been ordained as priest. My Bishop called me out of a retreat and knelt beside me, asking me to hear his confession. To cut a long story short, I forgot the prayer of absolution; I was tense and uncomfortable hearing the confession of the one, whose priesthood I shared, who mediated to me, the faculty, to hear confession. However, this event left a lasting impression on me regarding the need to be humble enough to make regular confession.

After the baptism of Jesus, the Father opened His heaven again (which was locked against Adam). He sent His Spirit, which hovered over creation, to restore order. The Spirit came like a dove, reminding us of the dove which announced to Noah, the end of God's wrath. The Father spoke again as He spoke in the beginning.

Seeing this, the baptism of Jesus now begins to make sense. Jesus' baptism is significant in these ways:

I. He was baptised not to be cleansed by the water, but to cleanse, purify and consecrate the water of baptism. He Himself is the Water of Life (Ezekiel 47, John 4:14, 7:37, 1 Corinthians 10:4) that brought life to the water of baptism.

II. The baptism of Jesus is a deepening of His incarnation. He accepted it, not as a necessity, but in solidarity with humanity, which He had come to save. He identified with us in every way.

III. By accepting baptism, He took our sins upon Himself and washed them in the river of Jordan, so that we can take upon ourselves His righteousness. It was a vicarious action (Isaiah 53:12).

IV. He accepted baptism in order to teach us, by example, the necessity of baptism.

V. He accepted baptism in obedience to God because God had willed it to be an occasion of epiphany; to reveal Jesus to the world as His begotten Son, an affirmation that John himself would need to strengthen his faith when he would be arrested six months later.

Today, dear friends, let us associate with John. We can relate to his reluctance because he never understood what God had in mind; he never understood why Jesus should be baptised and so he tried to debate this.

Often, we are in John's situation. I wager that many people in the Church will understand what I am talking about right now; those times when we can't understand what God is doing, why He is doing what He is doing and the way He is doing it; the times when we don't understand why God would say No to an important request; those moments when we cannot explain why a particular thing should happen to us or to someone who is faithful to God; or perhaps those times when God asks us to do something and we don't understand why we should and we don't even want to. There are times when God has asked me to forgive and be reconciled with people I would rather not have to relate with ever again.

The Magi didn't understand why God told them not to go back to Herod, why they were warned to go another way that they weren't even familiar with. Elizabeth did not understand why she was barren for so long despite her faith and faithfulness. The sisters of Lazarus did not understand why their brother, the friend of Jesus should die just like that.

My message today is that we may not understand it all and to be honest with you, we are not meant to understand everything, but if we understand and accept this, then it is enough:

God has reasons for everything He does, everything He permits to happen in our lives, everything He asks us to do. It may not make sense to us as, it did not make sense to John today, but at the end, God always makes perfect sense.

Blessed Cyprian Iwene Tansi, Priest

Feast (For the Church in Nigeria)

READING TEXTS: *Philippians 2: 1-11; Resp: Isaiah 12; Matthew 13: 44-46*

Today, we celebrate the memorial of one of our very own, Blessed Cyprian Iwene Tansi.

Blessed Cyprian was born in September 1903 at Aguleri in Anambra, Nigeria. He was a Son of a pagan father. His Father sent him to a Catholic School and there he became a Catholic and was baptised Michael.

He eventually became a teacher, a catechist and was later ordained a priest on the 19th December 1937. He worked so hard in many parishes in Nigeria.

As a priest, he lived a very austere life, unlike the luxurious and comfortable lives many missionaries sought and lived at that time. He was a reformer wherever he worked. He was so kind to people and down to earth. He encouraged education among natives, stood up against prevalent sexual immoralities, preached and fought for peace, and sought to purge everything in the culture that contradicted the Gospel spirit, for instance the cult of masquerades, injustice against women etc.

Later in 1950, he became a Cistercian monk at St. Bernard Monastery, England. There he lived a simple life, totally dedicated to God in prayer, humility and love. He fell ill and was diagnosed of a coronary aneurism. He died 2 weeks later on 20th January 1964 in Leicester.

12

He was beatified by Pope John Paul II on the 22nd March 1998.

Lessons for Christ's faithful

Blessed Tansi reminds us that we are all called to be saints. Only saints are in heaven and so if you want to make heaven, make effort to be a saint. Without holiness no one can see God (Hebrews 12:14).

Blessed Tansi reminds us that it is possible to be a saint in our present circumstances and time. He lived in a very difficult time too; when Christianity was unpopular, when immorality was on the increase, and yet he never lost focus.

Practical lessons from his life

*I.	Humility*

St Paul enjoins us to imbibe humility using Christ as a model. We see this in Blessed Tansi. He was a Priest, like a small god and yet he was down to earth, was not inflated by the prestige of his privileged position. He even lived in mud houses, rode on bicycles and often trekked long distances. He didn't think too high of himself or too low of other people. He was a humble man. Piety without humility is hypocrisy.

*II.	Sincerity of intention*

St Paul tells us to do nothing out of selfishness or conceit. Many black people wished to become priests at the time of Tansi, simply because they believed the priesthood guaranteed them comfort, luxury and enviable status. The life of Tansi reveals that his interest was not carnal, selfish or mean. He aspired to the Priesthood to serve God and God's people. As for you, always question your motives for seeking what you seek, for doing what you do, for desiring what you desire. A good deed is often poisoned by wrong intention.

III. Beacon of Unity

Blessed Tansi was known as a peacemaker, an agent of unity and love in every parish he worked. St Paul tells the Philippians today, *"complete my joy by being of the same mind, having the same love, being in full accord and of one mind."* Dear friends, let us all be committed to upholding unity; let us be agents of love and accord. Most of our communities, families, groups, pious associations and even friends today are torn apart by malice and division. Most of these are caused by unnecessary issues, simple matters, avoidable quibbles, petty quarrels that could have been simply resolved by being more Christian. Unfortunately, we allow simple matters to separate us; we allow time to cement the severity, our hardness of heart makes resolution difficult and the situation stifles the overflow of grace among us. What a pity.

Through the prayers of Blessed Tansi, may God teach us to be humble, to be properly motivated and to be passionate for unity.

Amen.

The Conversion of St. Paul, Apostle
Feast

———❦❦❦———

READING TEXTS:
Acts 22:3-16; Psalm 117; Mark 16:15-18

Today, the Church celebrates the feast of the conversion of St. Paul. This is a historic event with profound significance and that is why it is being celebrated annually in the Church.

Whenever we celebrate this feast, we take a reading that recalls the story of the conversion of St. Paul. He was a fierce persecutor of Christianity, but the light of truth shone on him and he became an ardent defender of what he once tried to eliminate.

Today, we will reflect on these two points:

I.   Revelation for divine direction

Saul persecuted the Christians, not out of *deliberate malice,* but out of *ignorant zeal* for God. He was too sure he was defending the purity of true religion (Judaism); but when God opened his eyes he saw through God's eyes. He discovered he was wrong. He had been opposing God, whom he set to defend.

Sometimes we also think we are on the path of righteousness. We think we are working for God and walking with God. We think God is pleased with us. We think it is well with us. We think we are in the right vocation, relationship and location but then we may be wrong (read Revelation 3:17).

15

Let today's feast move us to pray daily that the Lord opens our eyes to see as we are seen, to cure us of all spiritual blindness, ignorance and error in our lives, and to direct us in the right path always.

II. The role of Ananias

God called Ananias and used him to help Saul to move from a wrong road to the right way, to move from ignorance to the truth and from false living to finding Life (Jesus).

Today, there are so many 'Sauls' in our world; people who need help to find Jesus. Some do not even recognise their need for Jesus. These are people who are running hard and innocently on the path of condemnation. God needs us to help bring people from error to truth, from slavery of sin to freedom in Christ, from darkness to light, from hopelessness to Christ, the hope of glory.

That is what the Gospel of today summons us to do: to accept the ministry of Ananias; to lead 'Sauls' to Christ.

I propose we start with daily prayers and offerings for unbelievers, persecutors of the faith, for hardened sinners, for enemies of the Church, for all living in ignorance, darkness and deception.

Pray also that the Lord will open our eyes to see the 'Sauls' around us. As we pray, remember to also WATCH.

The Presentation of the Lord

Feast

READING TEXTS: *Malachi 3:1-4; Psalm 24; Hebrews 2:14-18; Luke 2:22-40*

Dearly beloved in the Lord, today is exactly forty days since we celebrated the birth of Jesus. According to the Jewish custom (Leviticus 12:3-8; Exodus 13:2, 12, 15), forty days after the birth of a child, the mother is purified and if the child is the first-born son, he is presented and redeemed. So today we celebrate the feast of the presentation of the Lord in the temple and the purification of Mary.

The feast of today contains several biblical paradoxes and I will enunciate a few.

The parents of Jesus were not rich enough to afford the prescribed lamb, so they brought a pair of turtledoves (see Leviticus 12:1-8, especially verse 8). However, in actual fact, they offered the best of lambs to God, because the child they brought was the Lamb of God Himself, the Lamb that God Himself approved and supplied.

They brought Jesus to the temple to be consecrated but, in actual fact, He is the Temple of God whose presence consecrated the Jewish Temple.

Jesus was ceremoniously presented/dedicated to God, whereas, in actual fact, He was the one presenting and dedicating us to God in Himself.

17

In appearance, Simeon held Jesus in his arms but in reality, He holds Simeon. He holds us, and the whole world, in His arms.

There are at least four characters that have an important place in today's feast:

I.   The parents of Jesus, who were committed and devout Jews.
II. Jesus Himself, who shared in our human condition and experiences. The presentation is a prolongation of His incarnation, a deepening of His solidarity with us.
III. Simeon, who was a devout and righteous man.
IV. Anna, a widow who consecrated her life to God and spent it in prayer and fasting.

Today, I will reflect on Simeon's experience and draw just two lessons.

I.   Simeon waited on the Lord

We are told that it had been revealed to Simeon that he would not see death until he had set his eyes on the Christ.

From the moment of the promise, Simeon had been waiting, anticipating and preparing for the fulfilment of that promise. He had waited for years and decades. Even when he became so advanced in age, probably over a hundred years, he was still hoping for the promised Saviour. Today's feast is a celebration of God's faithfulness to His promise. God fulfilled in His own time, the promise He had made to Simeon.

Maybe there is someone here like Simeon; waiting for something to happen; waiting for something to change; waiting for clarity and direction. Someone here is waiting for his/her prayers to be answered. Here is God's message for you: continue to trust the promise, do not despair and do not walk away from the promise.

Habakkuk 2:3 says: *still the vision awaits its appointed time; it hastens to the end   it will not lie. If it seems slow, wait for it; it will surely come...*

II.   Simeon's eyes were opened

Simeon was a man advanced in age; probably his eyesight was beginning to fail him. Today, Simeon saw more than the human eye could see. Human eyes saw a forty days-old baby, yet Simeon saw salvation; people saw a crying infant, yet Simeon saw a light to enlighten the Gentiles; he saw the glory of Israel. It was another epiphany for Simeon.

How was Simeon able to see this? The Gospel of today is clear regarding the actions of the Holy Spirit on Simeon. It says the Holy Spirit rested on him; it was revealed to him by the Holy Spirit; he was prompted by the Holy Spirit.

Ephesians 1:8: Paul prayed that the eyes of our minds be opened. We need to ask the Holy Spirit to open our eyes too, to enable us to see the mysteries that the human eye is incapable of capturing.

In Numbers 22:22-31, we have the account of how an Angel stood in front of Balaam, yet he never saw it, whereas his donkey saw and cowered in terror; until the Lord opened Balaam's eyes to see.

When we see with only our physical eyes, we miss so much. One of the places where we miss so much is at the Mass. At every Mass, heaven unites with earth; Jesus is presented again in the temple; the altar becomes Calvary. The Mass can also be an epiphany.

Sadly, only those enlightened by the Holy Spirit can see this and so I pray that, like Simeon, the Holy

Spirit will open our spiritual eyes to see the miracles of God that surround us always; most especially when we come to offer the supreme sacrifice of the Mass.

Today is also the world day of consecrated life established by Pope John Paul II. We keep in our prayers all men and women who have consecrated themselves to serve God in poverty, chastity, obedience and prayer.

St. Cyril and St. Methodius, Bishops
Memorial

READING TEXTS:
Acts 13:46-49; Psalm 117; Luke 10:1-9

Today is the 14th February and the Church in Europe celebrates the feast of her co-patrons St. Cyril and St. Methodius. They were Byzantine Christian theologians and they were also missionaries. They were sent as missionaries to Moravia to preach the faith. They encountered and endured all forms of challenge, but they were courageous men of deep faith and unwavering missionary vision.

They invented the Glagolithic alphabets to foster the education and evangelisation of the Slavs. They translated the Bible and the liturgical texts into the Slavonic language. They were given the title of Apostles of the Slavs. Pope John Paul II, in 1980, declared them co-patrons of Europe with St Benedict of Nursia.

As we reflect on the missionary zeal and apostolic vision of Saints Cyril and Methodius, the readings of today evoke in us a sense of mission too. We see Paul and Barnabas in the First reading fulfilling their mandate as missionaries, not just to the Jews, but to the Gentiles too.

In the Gospel, we have the account of Jesus sending out seventy-two others, with a sense of urgency to preach the Good News of God's Kingdom; to be agents of peace and healing wherever they were sent.

Putting all this together, we are being reminded that it is not enough for us to be disciples; the essence of discipleship is apostleship. The essence of being with the Lord is so that He might send us out also (Mark 3:14). Our faith, piety and devotion have not fulfilled their ultimate end until we reach out to others.

The Lord is reminding us today that each of us here is a missionary; each of us is a messenger of peace; each of us is a teacher of the faith; each of us has received the power to minister God's grace and healing using the authority of Christ. We are sent, like Cyril and Methodius, like Paul and Barnabas, like the seventy-two.

Let us pray today that the Lord will use our lives, words, hands and examples, to minister faith, joy, truth, peace, healing and salvation to others.
Amen.

The See of St. Peter, Apostle

Feast

— ❧❦❧ —

READING TEXTS:
1 Peter 5:1-4; Psalm 23; Matthew 16:13-19

Today, the Holy Mother Church celebrates the feast of the Chair of St. Peter.

This feast recalls how Christ named the Galilean fisherman the shepherd of His flock and gave him the authority of a teacher and guide of His Church. This is what we have just heard in today's Gospel. In the First Reading, we have St. Peter exercising his teaching and governing authority by exhorting the other elders of Christian communities to be wise and faithful shepherds/stewards.

On a day like this, we are to reflect on the supremacy of the office of the Pope as the Vicar of Christ and the visible head of the Church of Christ. We are being reminded of the need to pray for the Pope, always.

It's a challenging office. A great burden rests on his shoulders; a lot of pressure and temptation. He is a special target of the devil and the devil's agents. The Pope is a pastor, a father, a leader, a teacher and a judge over the universal Church, and yet he is human.

It is very easy and common these days for people to criticise the Pope and say all kinds of calumny against him, but we must always be reminded that our responsibility is primarily to support the Vicar of Christ

23

with our prayers, love and good will. Most of the ill-feelings against the Pope are based on 'half-truths', gleaned without knowing the whole truth.

I think that this is exactly what the devil wants: for the faithful to be opposed to their head; a household divided against itself. We may not always want to agree with the Pope, but he remains the Vicar of Christ. He might at times be weak and impetuous, like Peter, but he is the choice of God through the Holy Spirit.

Please, let us pray for the Pope. Let us pray daily for him. Let us pray that the devil will not succeed in bringing him down. Let us also pray against every negative inclination and sentiment towards him.

In addition, on a day like this, we reflect on our identity as Catholics. We are members of the Church that Christ established on the foundation of the Apostles. We enjoy the fullness of revealed truth, the fullness of the means of salvation; we have the apostolic heritage. Now, let us ask ourselves these three questions:

I.   *Do we love our Church?*

In the light of recent happenings in the Church, so many people (though still in the Church) have developed anti-ecclesiastical and anti-clerical sentiments. Today's feast reminds us that the Church is our Mother and we have no other; so, despite the weakness of her members and authorities, we are still called to love our Mother, cherish our faith, plant it in our children and encourage them to grow in it.

II. *Do we believe and follow what the Catholic Church teaches?*

Are we Catholics by identity but not by mentality? Are we Catholics who select what to believe? Some Catholics tell you they don't believe in infant baptism, they don't believe in purgatory, they don't say Hail Mary.

They even despise the Blessed Virgin Mary. Some don't believe in the Church's teaching on marriage and healthy family life. Some members of the Church do not even know what the Church teaches on very important moral issues and so they cannot follow it or teach them to others.

III.   Do we practice our faith?

There are some who claim to be Catholics and yet they do not practice the faith or practice it minimally.

They say no Angelus, no Rosary; they do not make confession. It does not 'appeal' to them to venerate Jesus in the Blessed Sacrament. If they are able to come on a Sunday, they watch the 'liturgical drama' with eyes always on their wristwatches and receive the 'white loaf', which is the reward of their mortifying presence with others; the rest is inconsequential.

Romans 9:6-7, *...for   not all Israelites truly belong to Israel, and not all of Abraham's children are his true descendants...*

We are Catholics not just by being physically present in the Church, but by being present with, to and for the Church, heart, mind and soul.

Ash Wednesday

READING TEXTS: *Joel 2:12-18; Psalm 51; 2 Corinthians 5:20-6:2; Matthew 6:1-6, 16-18*

Today we begin the holy season of Lent with the Ash Wednesday liturgy. We shall receive ashes on our foreheads, while these words are said to us:

> *Remember that you are dust and unto dust you shall return* (Genesis 3:19).
> or
> *Repent and believe in the Gospel* (Mark 1:15).

These are not flattering words. We do not want to be reminded that we are mortal; we do not like to be reminded of our failings and our need for repentance. But then, Lent is a season to remember and to repent.

The ashes we shall receive today will remind us of at least five things.

I.   Our originality

We are created by God, from the dust of the earth (Genesis 2:7). We did not will ourselves into existence and so we are not independent 'lords'; we are under the authority of our Creator.

II.   Our vanity

No matter how good and how beautiful we look, we are dust. Whatever is graceful and glorious in us comes only from God; what is underneath our beauty is being

26

put on our forehead today, to remind us that everything good in us comes from the Lord (Psalm 34:2; James 1:17; 2 Corinthians 3:5).

III.   Frailty and iniquity

As we receive ashes on our forehead, we are being reminded that we are all sinners, in need of mercy. Lent is a time for us to shift our focus from other people's lives, from their mistakes and misdeeds. It is a time to focus on ourselves; our sins, our need for forgiveness and grace.

A time to say, like the Psalmist, *my   offences truly I know them, my sin is always before me.*

So, the ashes we receive become a sign of our own contrition, not our anger at the fault of others, but our sorrow for our sins.

(Job 42:3-6; Jeremiah 6:26; Daniel 9:3; Jonah 3:6; Luke 10:13, Hebrews 9:13).

IV.   Mortality

These ashes remind us that our mortal lives shall end one day. Dust shall return to dust, ashes to ashes. There will come a day when my name will be called and I won't be in position to respond; a day when I will close my eyes and open it at the other side, in eternity. A day that will surely come.

This is a day we should always keep in mind and prepare for (Sirach 7:36).

V.   Reality of hell

Ashes are produced from the effect of fire. These ashes remind us of the reality of hell for all those who, by their own free will, rebelled against God; all those who reject His love and His offer of salvation. By rejecting God, they choose an eternity of separation from Him, in a place of eternal torment. No matter how post-modernism tries to make a myth out of hell, it is a reality and souls are languishing hopelessly there.

Thanks be to God that, by the sign of the Cross on our forehead, we are being reassured that through faith in the redemptive suffering and death of our Lord Jesus, we are freed from eternal damnation and shall rise again in glory to share with Christ the happiness of eternal life, which He won for us.

As we receive ashes today, let us see this season as an opportunity to remember the truth about who we really are and who we are called to be; to draw nearer to God through prayers, penance and alms giving.

PRAYER

Lord Jesus, I acknowledge that I am dust and ashes and whatever is good in me is evidence of your glory in me. Help me to live so that, when dust shall return to dust, what is immortal in dust shall not be deprived of your presence forever.

Amen.

St. David

Patron Saint of Wales (Feast)

WHAT DO I WANT IN LIFE?

READING TEXTS:
Philippians 3:8-14; Psalm 1:1-4,6;Matthew 5:13-16

I recently watching a program titled "Chosen." In that series, Jackie Francois interviewed a few people in Hollywood California, asking what they want in life?

Some people said they want to make enough money. A young man said all he cares about is to become famous. Someone said he wants his business to grow, and some people want a happy family and successful career. A few said happiness.

Maybe we can also start our reflection today by asking the same question, "What is most important to me in life? What are my priorities and motivations?

In today's reading, St. Paul gave his own answers. There are three things St. Paul wanted; they were his priority, motivation and vision.

I.   To know Jesus more and to experience the power of His resurrection.
II.   To live for the glory of God even if it involves sharing in Christ' suffering.
III. To be worthy of the prize which God has promised to all who are faithful to the end.

29

Wouldn't it be wonderful if these also become our priorities and motivations? To know Jesus more, to live for God's glory and to strive for eternal happiness.

In the Gospel of today, Jesus also touched on the issue of priority, motivation and vision. He tells us that our priority should be to make our lights shine and our motivation should be to give praise and glory to the Father.

Today is the feast of St. David. His priority was to live for God and His glory. He abandoned the world in pursuit of this, he became an abbot and later a Bishop.

St. David is credited with a monastic rule based on the example of the Eastern Fathers, and also with a Penitentiary. He was invited to preside at the synod of Llandewibrefi. Monks trained at his monastery, he evangelised South Wales and made foundations in Cornwall, Brittany and Ireland.

St. David is said to have sent a Mass rite to Ireland. At his death, his contemporary St. Kentigern, founder of St. Asaph's in North Wales, witnessed in vision his joyful entrance into the joy of his Lord. His holy relics have been found hidden in the fabric of St. David's Cathedral, where they are carefully preserved. He was canonized by Pope Callistus II in 1123.

Through his prayers, may God help us to set our priorities right; to be motivated by love of God and to focus our vision on eternal life with God.

St. Patrick, Bishop

Patron Saint of Ireland (Feast)
Second Patron of Nigeria (Feast)
———◦◦◦◦———

THE MIRACULOUS CATCH

READING TEXTS:
1 Peter 4:7-11; Psalm 96; Luke 5:1-11

Today, the Holy Mother Church celebrates the feast of St. Patrick, a very important figure in the Universal Church. He is the patron Saint of Ireland; he is also the Secondary Patron Saint of my country, Nigeria.

Let us begin our reflection from the Gospel of today. There is a wonderful TV series that presents the Gospel narrative in a very dramatic and compelling manner. It is entitled The Chosen and I recommend that we all try to watch it. In Episode 3 (The Rock On Which It Is Built), Peter was in trouble with the Roman authorities for being unable to pay his taxes. Matthew was sent to monitor him. Sadly, Peter was unable to catch any fish; which he needed to do, if he was to repay his debt on time.

However, as in today's Gospel, after using his boat, Jesus instructed him to, *put out his net into the deep water...* . Let us take note; Peter was in a very distressing situation; he did not know what to do. Jesus instructed him to do what appeared 'irrational'. Peter obeyed and then the story changed. The situation we may find ourselves in today is like that of Peter; we may be in difficult times and we may be feeling helpless and overwhelmed.

The question is: What is Jesus telling us today?

31

It is exactly what Jesus told Peter after the catch: Μὴφοβοὴ (mē phobou) that is *do not be afraid.* This is exactly what Jesus is telling us at this time. The miraculous catch today redirected Peter's focus, from his plight and fears, to the power of God. Today, Jesus wants us to also look beyond the issues of the world today, to the great power of God to help, save and redeem us.

Even the First Reading is apt. The Lord is saying something to us through St. Peter. Look at the opening line of the reading: *everything will soon come to an end, so, to pray better, keep a calm and sober mind.* At some point in their struggles, Peter and Andrew had to turn to their companions, James and John, to help them. Today, in the heart of Lent, in the middle of our fears, we are being reminded of St. Patrick, our friend, our companion, our brother in heaven.

St. Patrick, as we all know, was born in Great Britain around 385. As a young boy he was taken, as a captive (by Irish pirates), to Ireland. He worked for someone as a herdsman for six years, until his dramatic escape. Eventually, he felt called to the priesthood. He sensed the spiritual need of the people of Ireland and so he requested to return there to evangelise. There he was made a bishop.

Amidst heart-breaking challenges, St. Patrick recorded so much success that Ireland even began to send missionaries to other parts of the world. This day is also celebrated in Nigeria as a feast in recognition of the labours of Irish missionaries in the country.

As we seek God's face in the midst of our storms, as we seek to trust in God's power and obey His voice, telling us to come out of our fears and cast our net of faith, let us also turn to St. Patrick to pray to God for us and with us.

St. Joseph, Husband of Blessed Virgin Mary

Solemnity

—⟶∞⟵∞⟶—

READING TEXTS: *2 Samuel 7:4-5, 12-14, 16; Psalm 89; Romans 4:13, 16-18, 22; Matthew 1:16, 18-21, 24*

Dearly beloved in Christ, today we celebrate the solemnity of St. Joseph, the husband of the Blessed Virgin Mary and the foster-father of Jesus.

In the First Reading, we have the account of God's promises to David to establish his house forever. God fulfilled this by sending the Messiah through the house of David. Joseph is the link that connected Jesus to the house of David, although Mary most likely could have been also from the line of David; the New Testament is silent about this. Genealogy is traced through the paternal line.

There are three things I find very insightful about Joseph.

I. A man of honour

Joseph was described as a man of honour. This is something to ponder on. A person of honour is someone who respects himself/herself and others, and who is true in and to his word (honesty); a person who can be trusted; a person who avoids anything that has the form of evil or sin. The question is thus: am I a person of honour?

II. A trustworthy man

The Lord saw that He could trust Joseph and so entrusted to him the care of the Holy Family.

33

Recognising how Joseph fulfilled his divine mandate as the guardian of the Holy Family, the Church has entrusted herself to his care as the protector and patron of the Mystical Body of Christ. The questions are: Can the Lord trust me? Can He entrust to me something special to Him? What about everything the Lord has entrusted to me; do I prove myself worthy of trust?

III.   In the life of St. Joseph, we learn submission to God's will

It is very difficult to accept God's will when it is different from what we plan or desire. The whole mystery of the incarnation and virginal conception of Mary, accepting Mary and her pregnancy was never Joseph's plan.

However, he submitted to God's will. In life, the way to experience peace is not just to find comfort in prayers but to be open to God's will. Whatever God says and wills for us now, we should be ready to accept, otherwise, fear, anxiety and stress will rob us of a life of joy.

In conclusion, the pregnancy of Mary must have stressed Joseph in no small way but then the Lord spoke to him, gave him clarification and direction. These are the two things we need, now more than ever before.

In the world today, there is much to scare and worry us all. We do not know where we are heading. Let us seek the intercession of the protector of the Church, the patron of all families, so that through his prayers, we may receive clarification and direction in the midst of our widespread confusion and concern.

The Annunciation of the Lord
Solemnity
———❧❧❧———

READING TEXTS: *Isaiah 7:10-14; 8-10; Psalm 40; Hebrews 10:4-10; Luke 1:26-38*

Today is the 25th of March; it is exactly nine months to Christmas and the Holy Mother Church celebrates the Solemnity of the Annunciation of the Lord.

The Gospel of today explains what this means to us. The whole people of Israel have been praying for the Messiah to come, generation after generation expected the Messiah to come in their own time. Today, the Angel came to announce to Mary, a young Virgin, that the Messiah, Son of God and Son of David, shall come through her. She will become pregnant by the over shadowing of the Holy Spirit.

Two questions come to mind as I ponder this:

I.   Why didn't God just allow Mary to be fully married to Joseph and then bring the Messiah-child through their natural conjugal union? In that way there wouldn't be the threat of divorce or public embarrassment for either Joseph, Mary or the baby.

The answer is this. No one can dictate to God. He is not bound by our reasoning. His ways are not our ways. Often, we want to teach God how to govern His world or how to order our lives. We act as if we are special advisers to God. He needs no human advisers and will not conform to our methodical reasoning.

II. How can a child be conceived by the overshadowing of the Holy Spirit? This is unnatural. This is not a legitimate and conventional way of conceiving. Why has God chosen this way? Because God is not limited by nature; He does whatever He wills, when He wills and in the way He wills (Psalm 115:3).

This child is not just a child like any other child and so God's power must be manifested in His conception in a way that has never been and cannot be replicated.

The Angel explains this better: for nothing is impossible for God.

If this God is the God we serve, the God who can make a young girl conceive without intercourse, who told nature to be mute and commanded the ovaries of Elizabeth to produce an egg at menopause, then we cannot debate, doubt or contend with Him. We should just surrender and obey this God in all things.

This is what Mary did. Her response implies: Lord who am I to argue with you? Who am I to contend with your plans? Who am I to say No to You? Your wisdom is unsearchable, Your power is without bounds, You made me, and I belong to You; let what You have said be done to me.

This is the greatest expression of faith: Lord, I have no will except what You will; I have no objection to Your decision; I belong wholly and entirely to You; I cannot teach You how You should govern my life or suggest to You what to do with me; just do with me as You will.

This is what Ahaz does not understand. God sent the prophet Isaiah to him to trust that He will deliver him from Pekah, the King of Israel and Rezin, the King of Syria. But Ahaz could not figure out how that would happen, and he was firmly resolved to surrender to Tiglash-Pileser, King of Assyria. Ahaz argued with God and wanted his will to prevail and not God's will. This singular decision brought him ruin and destruction.

If we are only able to understand the God that we serve, we would stop doubting, complaining, blaming or arguing with Him. The response to such a God is: let whatever/everything you have said be done to me.

Palm Sunday

READING TEXTS: *Isaiah 50:4-7; Psalm 22; Philippians 2:6-11; Luke 22-23.*

Today is Palm Sunday, the beginning of the Holy Week when we celebrate the most significant events of our salvation. Today, we have a celebration that takes us through Christ's glorious entry into Jerusalem and His eventual arrest, condemnation and death.

As I prepared this reflection, so many themes came to my mind. For instance, the prayer of submission to God's will, which Jesus prayed at Gethsemane; the inability of Pilate to defend justice and truth; the denial of Peter; the request of the people for Barabbas and the demand for Jesus' death. I thought about reflecting on one of the powerful words of Jesus on the Cross of Calvary, or even the love of Joseph of Arimathaea.

Having prayed and reflected on all these, I feel in my spirit that God wants us to reflect on the sufferings of Jesus, as a consolation for us in our suffering. In the letter to the Hebrews 4:15, it is written:

> *For we do not have a high   priest who is unable to sympathise with our weaknesses; but one who in every respect has been tested as we are, yet without sin.*

Today, I will highlight five of the agonies of Jesus and we shall reflect on one.

38

I.   The betrayal of a brother and denial of a friend.
II.   False accusations.
III.   Physical torture and brutal treatment.
IV.   `Ingratitude of the beneficiaries of His Ministry of Mercy.
V.   He endured mockery on the Cross.

False accusations

Jesus was falsely accused. Being falsely accused brings about great pain, bitterness and sorrow. Many people today suffer unjust punishments, bad reputation and unfair treatment because of false accusations.

Some of us may also recall instances when we were falsely accused, when we were punished, discredited or ill-treated, even though we were innocent. Maybe someone here today, is going through the pain of false accusations and the associated consequences.

I once read the life-story of Joseph Richardson who, in 1967, was convicted of murdering his seven children, who all died after eating a meal tainted with powerful insecticide. Richardson was given the death sentence; this was later commuted to 25 years imprisonment. In 1988, a woman who occasionally acted as a babysitter for the Richardson children, Bessie Reese, confessed to the murder. Richardson was exonerated in 1989 after 22 years in prison. We can only imagine what this must have cost the innocent Joseph Richardson.

We have listened to the story of how some people emotionally, passionately and incessantly accused Jesus of inciting revolt, of opposing payment of tribute to Caesar and of planning a coup to make Himself a king. We have heard how they labelled Him a political agitator.

What, then, is Jesus saying to us today?

I. People may not understand our pains; people may not believe us, but Jesus says: I understand what you are going through; I went through it too.

II. Jesus is saying, learn from my reactions; I did not curse or insult my accusers (First Reading), I prayed for them. I committed my life and my cause to God; this is what I want you to do. This is where peace lies. Bitterness and hatred will not do your soul any good..

III. Jesus is saying to all of us, that as much as we dread the anguish of false accusations, let us also be resolved from today to be very slow to accuse others. Let us be careful in what we believe and say about people; we might be wrong, they might be innocent; we might be sinning against justice, humanity and charity.

God does not want us to join the crowd in accusing the innocent.

Holy Thursday

READING TEXTS: *Exodus 12:1-8, 11-14; Psalm 116; 1 Corinthians 11:23-26; John 13:1-15*

This week is the most solemn and glorious week in Christianity; it is the pinnacle of the liturgical year. In it we commemorate the final week of our Lord's life.

Holy Week begins with Palm Sunday and culminates with Easter Sunday. As Holy Week progresses to its final days, the solemnity heightens. The most solemn days of the Holy Week are the last three days called the Paschal Triduum; these days recount Jesus' last three days on earth. The days are Holy Thursday, Good Friday, and the climax of the Holy Saturday vigil. It ends with evening prayers on Easter Sunday.

Today, being Holy/Maundy Thursday, is the first day of the Paschal Triduum.

Today's Mass is referred to as the Mass of the Lord's Supper. At this Mass the Church relives and celebrates the institution of the Holy Eucharist (the Holy Sacrifice of the Mass at the last supper), as well as the institution of the Holy priesthood. This took place the evening before Jesus suffered and was crucified.

These Sacraments were instituted within the context of the Jewish Passover celebration. Jesus gave the Passover meal a new meaning. He changed the bread and wine to His body and blood. He gave them His body

41

and blood 'sacramentally' today, and by, tomorrow, He will give them 'actually'.

After the homily today, there shall be the ceremony of the washing of feet. This is a remembrance of Jesus' act as we have it in today's Gospel, and a demonstration of the priesthood as a call to service in love and humility.

This Mass concludes with the procession of the Blessed Sacrament to the altar of repose. This brings to mind the prayer and agony of Jesus in the garden of Gethsemane and His eventual arrest tonight. We are all expected to stay with Jesus in adoration and prayer.

As we take part in this liturgical celebration, let us keep these three points in mind.

I.   Jesus Himself instituted the sacrament of the priesthood; He made humans His representatives and defined their ministry. The primary ministry of the priest is to continue to offer the sacred Body and Blood of Christ in the sacrifice of the Mass, and to be a representative of Jesus in the world.

There is the temptation to forget that priests are Vicars of Christ, especially in the wake of recent scandals and regrettable events in the Church.

However, we must not lose sight of the fact that priests, though weak, remain Christ's representatives here on earth. The Lord wants us to honour Him in them, to pray for them and to support them positively to be able to discharge their responsibilities in piety, charity, humility and joy. They may be weak, but Christ loves them, and He chose them, and we must love, accept, respect, support and pray for them. Whatever we do to any priest, we do to Christ.

II. As we also recall the institution of the Holy Eucharist, it is an opportunity to be grateful to God for this great sacrament; this most Holy Sacrament of life, love and grace; the sacrament that has changed the lives of many of us and is still changing lives today.

We are also invited to re-examine our lives. How well do we revere these wondrous gifts? Do we believe in the presence of Jesus in the Holy Eucharist? Do we receive Jesus with reverence and awe? Do we prepare ourselves to receive Jesus worthily? Do we honour His sacramental presence in our midst? Do we reflect in our lives, what we receive into our bodies?

III. As we watch Jesus washing His disciples' feet, we are to examine our lives too. How humble am I? How loving to others am I? How willing am I to be of service to my brothers and sisters in their need? Do I wash other people's feet too, or put dust/thorns in their paths?

May our participation in these most solemn events be for us an opportunity of grace, repentance and salvation.

Good Friday

READING TEXTS: *Isaiah 52:13-53:12; Psalm 31; Hebrews 4:14-16, 5:7-9; John 18:1-19:42*

Today is a solemn day of mourning, fasting and prayer. A day when we celebrate the Lord's passion and death.

The liturgy is divided into three principal parts:

I. *The Liturgy of the Word*
    In the First Reading, the prophet Isaiah explained to us the vicarious suffering of Christ. He suffered for us: He was wounded for us; He died for us. The letter to the Hebrews explained that through His suffering, He has become the source of eternal salvation to us all. The Gospel is the passion narrative according to St. John's account.
    The Liturgy of the Word ends with solemn intercessions.

II. *The adoration of the Cross*
    Today, we shall all adore the Cross of Christ; the symbol of shame that, by the power of God, became the sign of glory, victory, power and a defeat of the devil.

III. *The reception of Holy Communion*
    The ceremony concludes with the reception of Holy Communion. We receive into our souls sacramentally, what Jesus offered actually on the Cross today - His Body.

What is good about today?

When something unpleasant happens to us, we call the day a 'bad day'. Today, the greatest tragedy happened; the strangest and saddest news was heard - the Son of God breathed His last; He passed on. What news!

I remember 31August 1997; the world was cold and silent because Princess Diana died. On 10 January 2016, there was much sadness after a musician, David Bowie, breathed his last. These days are remembered as sorrowful days.

Paradoxically, today, the day the Son of God died, is called Good Friday; correctly so, it is a 'Good Friday.

This is the message. There are some things that may appear to us as tragedy, as signs of God's abandonment; some things are enough to make us cry: *My   God! My God!! Why have you forsaken me?*

Unknown to us, what appears bad is actually evidence of God's love and goodness in disguise. The death of Jesus is an example of such. It sounds like bad news, but it is in fact the news of our redemption.

But before Jesus died, I noticed how He gave away everything He had.

He first handed over the mantle of leadership to Peter. Yesterday, He shared His priestly office and authority with the disciples. He gave them His body and blood in a sacramental manner. Today, He gave His clothes to the soldiers to share; He gave His Mother to John the Beloved; He also gave all His beloved disciples, to His Mother. He gave His body for all of us on the Cross.

What is left? His spirit! This He gave to the Father: *into your hands Lord, I commend my Spirit.*

Jesus gave all for us. He gave all to come to us. He left all to go back to the Father.

There are three important questions to ask ourselves today.

I. How grateful am I for the love of Jesus for me and how grateful am I to the one who has sacrificed His life in order that I may have life?
II. What am I going to give, in return, to Jesus for this excess love?
III. What am I willing to sacrifice to bring joy, meaning and happiness to others?

Holy Saturday

READING TEXTS:
1. *Genesis 1:1- 2:2;psalm 104:1-2a, 5-6, 10, 12, 13-14, 24, 35c*
2. *Genesis 22:1-18; Psalm 16:5, 8, 9-10, 11*
3. *Exodus 14:15-15:1;psalm: Exodus 15:1b-2, 3-4, 5-6, 17-18*
4. *Isaiah 54:5-14; Psalm 30:2, 4, 5-6,11-12a, 13b*
5. *Isaiah 55:1-11; Psalm 12:2-3,4bcde, 5-6*
6. *Baruch 3:9-15, 32-4:4; Psalm 19:8 - 11*
7. *Ezekiel 36:16-17a, 18-28, Psalm 42:3,5bcd, 43:3-4*
8. *Romans 6:3-11; Psalm 118:1-17, 22-23.*
    ***Gospel: Year A:** Matthew 28:1-10*
       ***Year B:** Mark 16:1-7*
       ***Year C:** Luke 24:1-12*

At Christmas, we sing Silent Night, Holy Night, but today is the most silent, most Holy and solemn night. Today is the vigil of all vigils. Today the Church celebrates her best, most beautiful, most dramatic liturgy.

My reflection will be divided into three:

I.   The meaning of this night.
II. The liturgy of tonight.
III. The message of today.

I.   The meaning of this night

On Good Friday, Jesus was falsely accused, unjustly condemned, beaten, scourged, mocked, crucified, died and was buried in the tomb. While His body lay in the tomb, His spirit went to perform the last

47

phase of His Messianic mission. In the Spirit, He fought and conquered death. He went to open the gates of Hades for the righteous souls who died before Him, that they may enter into heaven (1 Peter 3:18-19). After this, He rose victorious from the grave. So, we are celebrating the night when Jesus defeated death and rose again from the grave.

II.   The liturgy of tonight

The liturgy of this night is divided into four parts:

i.   The 'Lucernarium' or service of light

This takes us back to the beginning of time, when the whole world was a formless void (Genesis 1:2), engulfed in meaningless darkness. God was the only light. His glory was like a consuming fire (Exodus 24:17). We light the Paschal candle from the mighty fire to impress on us that Jesus is light from light, true God from true God.

In the middle of the Church, we light our candles too and we help others to light theirs from ours. This is to indicate that those who follow Jesus will no longer be in darkness (John 8:12) but will shine and become light to others (Matthew 5:14). This service of light ends with the Easter praise. Once enlightened by Christ, our lives should be a hymn of praise to God until we shall praise Him for all eternity in Heaven.

ii.   Liturgy of the Word

We read the story of God's relationship with humankind, which culminates in the salvation of humanity; a story of God's undying love for us; a love that brought about what we celebrate tonight.

iii. Renewal of baptismal promises

The third part is baptism or renewal of baptismal promises. The liturgy of baptism reminds us of the connection between baptism and the resurrection. In baptism we enter into the mystery of Christ's death and resurrection and are made sharers in the fruits of His redemptive death (Romans 6:4, Colossians 2:12).

iv. Liturgy of the Eucharist

In the joy of resurrection, Christ invites us to the table with Him, with the hope that one day we shall rise again with Him to new life where we shall partake in the Eternal Paschal feast.

III. The message of today

The liturgy of today records so many transitions; from darkness to light, silence to praises, from being sober to being joyful, from Lent to the joy of Easter, from the grave to new life.

The Lord wants a transition to take place in our lives as well, and He wants it to begin from tonight. He wants us to move from our darkness and the graves, to light and new life. Our darkness and our graves represent any aspect of our lives, our relationship, our job, our habit, character, our resolution and any plan that doesn't glorify God. We must move away from them.

What are those things in our lives that do not glorify God? This is what you will need to identify with the help of the Holy Spirit and, with the help of the same Holy Spirit, begin to disengage from decisively, and have a new life with the risen Lord.

Easter Sunday

Solemnity

───❦───

LIVING THE RESURRECTION LIFE

READING TEXTS:
Acts 10:34, 37-43; Psalm 118; Colossians 3:1-4; John 20:1-9

Today is a special day. Well, every day is special as long as God lives in us. It is the day of the resurrection. We started with the vigil, and we continue to savour this joy, not only through Easter, but through our lives. There are so many themes in my mind to reflect on today. However, let us reflect on living the resurrection life.

Through our Lenten journey, we have suffered, died and were buried with Jesus. Now He has risen to a new life. He was dead and He is now alive into the new life of the resurrection. We too are being invited to begin to live the new life of the resurrection.

What is the new life of resurrection?

I. *The resurrection life is a new life of joy.*

Joy in the midst of my challenges; joy that comes from knowing that God is in charge and all things are working for our good.

II. *It is living without fear of death.*

Death causes a very great fear and it can be seen as the worst evil, the greatest enemy of life. Yet with Christ's resurrection, death has been swallowed up in victory. Death can no longer hold us. By His dying and His rising, He has destroyed death. In rising He has restored to us the hope of immortality. When we die, we shall rise to a new life with Jesus (John 11:25-26; 1 Corinthians 15:55-57).

III. It is a life that looks towards heaven.

The resurrection life is a life lived in a way that ensures we don't allow our lives to be dictated and controlled by the passing things of this world. It is to live in this world constantly looking unto God and His heavenly promises. It is living in this world and yet reminding ourselves that this world is not our own; our treasures are in heaven. It is not resting our hope, joy and consolation in the things of the world. This is one of the important lessons I learnt from the destruction, by fire, of the magnificent cathedral in France (Colossians 3:1-4).

IV. The resurrection life is a new life of hope.

It is believing that all things are possible with God; believing that no matter what people have said or done, God has the final say. If life can emerge from the grave, our lives and situations are never hopeless. We will not listen to the devil. We will stay in faith because we are serving a God who can bring out life from the tomb.

V. The resurrection life is a new life of grace.

It is leaving behind old habits of sin, lifestyles of sin. It is leaving our corruption and embracing an incorruptible life with God. It is a new habit, lifestyle and character; a new vision of life, attitude, perspective and perception. It is nailing our sins to the Cross, with Jesus, burying our old self with Him and rising to newness with Him (2 Corinthians 5:17).

VI. It is a life of victory

The resurrection life is to live with the assurance of victory. We should not live our lives like defeated people. Jesus has conquered for us; we are victorious in Him. Romans 8:37 tells us, *in   all things we are more than conquerors....*

We cannot go through life as victims; suppressed, oppressed or depressed. We are co-conquerors with Jesus over the devil, over sin, over principalities and powers, over the enemies of our salvation, by the power of the victory already won (Colossians 2:15).

Dear friends, Christ is inviting us today to a new life, to the resurrection life; to life outside the tomb. He is inviting us to a life of joy, a life free from fear of death, a redeemed lifestyle, a life of victory, a new life of hope and grace. Alleluia! Praise you Our Lord Jesus Christ. **Amen.**

Divine Mercy Sunday

— ❧❧❧ —

GODLY ATTITUDE TOWARDS AN UNBELIEVER

READING TEXTS: *Acts 5:12-16; Psalm 118; Revelation 1:9-13, 17-19; John 20:19-31*

Today, we shall be reflecting on an issue so sensitive and very important; a reality that affects virtually every one of us here, beginning with me. We shall be reflecting on the 'Godly attitude to an unbelieving friend or family'.

One very pressing intention of many of us, is that God should restore some of our friends, family members, colleagues to the faith. One of the deepest pains many of us have is seeing people we love not believing in God or practicing their faith; a faith that has become the centre of your own life and joy.

Another related matter is the fact that some people whom we see practicing the faith are not really convinced. Many people practice the faith today to make their parents, spouses or family happy, but deep within, there is no life or understanding.

Sometimes we also struggle with our faith.

What today's Gospel tells us

In the Gospel of today, Jesus appeared to the disciples, showed them His hands and side and breathed the Holy Spirit on them, so that they would become ambassadors of His mercy.

It happened that Thomas was not there. Thomas, by his absence, represents all those who absent themselves or who have separated themselves from the assembly of God's children. When the disciples told him that Jesus is risen and that He has appeared to them, he refused to believe their testimony/arguments (like those who do not believe in our God and the truth of our faith).

For eight days, he was not convinced. He was unmoved by their celebrations and meditations; all he wanted was his own personal experience. Only after eight long days of the Church praying for him and tolerating his disbelief, did Jesus re-appear. He cleared the doubts of Thomas. Thomas, who once doubted and separated himself from the community of believers, after the encounter with Jesus, professed the profoundest faith in Christ's divinity and he wasted no time in taking the message of the Gospel as far as India, where he was martyred.

What is Jesus saying to us today?

I.   Jesus is saying that we really shouldn't go through life blaming ourselves for someone's loss of faith. There are many things that can be responsible for loss of faith.

II.   Do not treat anyone with hatred, scorn or intolerance because of their lack of interest in the faith, or because they have abandoned the Church. These dispositions can only harden them more. God doesn't hate anyone for not believing in Him. Do not become more passionate for God than God demands.

III.   You can't force anyone to accept and practice faith. Monica once drove Augustine out of her home for abandoning the faith, but it never worked. We may also need to learn that our best arguments may not be enough to persuade anyone. Often, what people need is an experience of God that will change them completely.

What should I do?

I. Witness to the beauty of your faith through a life of constant joy, faith and peace. Even in the crises of life, show a joyful celebration of your faith, through a character of grace, and through sincere love and kindness to people.

It is unfortunate that many of those who do not even practice the faith, demonstrate greater virtue than some of us. Many people are discouraged because of the hypocrisy of the people of faith. The First Reading tells us that the early believers drew many unbelievers to the faith through the witness of their lives.

II. Pray unceasingly and with faith for them. An unceasing prayer of faith for the conversion of an unbeliever will never be wasted; it may happen sooner or later, but it will restore them some day in God's own way.

Many of them are seeking meaning; many are having experiences that are very challenging. Some are asking questions that they haven't found answers to, many are longing for an experience of God.

III. Finally, today is Divine Mercy Sunday, a very unique day to present to Jesus all those who are separated from the Church, and all those who do not believe in God.

These souls are dear to Jesus. On the fifth day of the Divine Mercy Novena, Jesus says to St. Faustina:

Today, bring to me those who do not believe in God and those who do not yet know me. I was thinking of them during my bitter passion, and their future zeal comforted my heart. Immerse them in the ocean of my mercy.

Let us immerse today, in the ocean of mercy, all those who have deviated from the faith, all those who do not yet know the Lord or understand the meaning and beauty of our faith, and all those not convinced about their faith. Trusting in God's mercy, we know that many souls will have a life changing experience of God today through our fervent prayers.

23 APRIL

St. George

Patron Saint of England (Solemnity)

READING TEXTS: *Apocalypse 12:10-12: Psalm 126; Romans 5:1-5; John 15:18-21*

Today we celebrate the Solemnity of St. George, the Patron Saint of England.

Each nation has her own "patron saint", whose intercession is sought always as a specific helper to that nation. St. David is the patron saint of Wales, St. Andrew, of Scotland, St. Patrick, of Ireland, whilst St. George is the patron of England.

St. George was a high-ranking officer in the Roman army, who was able to combine his faith with his career. Emperor Diocletian had him tortured to make him deny his faith in Christ. Despite all the terrible torture, St. George showed incredible courage and faith. He was finally beheaded near Lydda in Palestine.

His martyrdom converted about 40,900 pagans to Christianity, including the empress Alexandra.

There is a golden legend of St. George and the dragon. It tells of how St. George killed a fierce dragon that was causing panic in the city of Silene, Libya. The people sacrificed two sheep each day to the dragon and later they started sacrificing humans. St. George saved the king's daughter by slaying the dragon with a lance. St. George offered the treasures given to him by the king to the poor. The people of the town were amazed, and most became Christians.

King Richard I of England placed his crusading

57

army under the protection of St. George, and in 1222 his feast was proclaimed a holiday.

King Edward III made him the patron Saint of England when he formed the order of the Garter in St. George's name in 1350, and the cult of St. George was further advanced by King Henry V, at the battle of Agincourt in Northern France.

There are two lessons from St. George's life.

I.   He was a soldier and yet a saint.

Our career should never be an impediment to our Christian life. We are called to be holy in whatever state of life we are. We should be careful that our career, profession, associations, ambitions in life do not stand against us and our Christian conscience and our commitment to God.

II.   St. George chose death rather than disobey God.

He chose to disobey the emperor rather than offend God. The First Reading describes to us those who are conquerors. They triumph over the fiercest dragon by the blood of the Lamb, and by the witness of their martyrdom, because even in the face of death, they did not cling to life.

This is the kind of zeal we have seen in the believers of the early Church. They were ready to risk their lives to obey God. Rescued from prison, they did not run away but continued to fulfil the mandate of the Lord.

We need the help of the Holy Spirit to be able to be faithful to God under certain circumstances and to be able to overcome fear, especially when what we cherish the most is being threatened. So, we pray today for a fresh experience of the power of the Holy Spirit.

We pray also that St. George may continue to intercede for our country, England.

St. George... Pray for us.

St. Mark, Evangelist

Feast

—————————

READING TEXTS: *1 Peter 5:5-14; Psalm 89:2-7, 16-17; Mark 16:15-20*

Today, the Holy Mother Church celebrates the feast of St. Mark. St. Mark was a cousin and disciple of St. Barnabas and St. Paul. He later became a disciple and interpreter for St. Peter. He interpreted Peter's preaching in Aramaic into Greek and Latin. He wrote down the sermons of Peter about Jesus and that is what we have today, as the Gospel account of Jesus from St. Mark. He wrote this for Gentile Christians in Rome. The Gospel captured the core and essence of the ministry of Jesus without being detained by details. His Gospel was helpful in the compilation of Matthaen and Lucan accounts too.

In AD 49, he travelled to Alexandria and founded the first Church in Alexandria. He became the first Bishop of Alexandria. There he was martyred by being dragged through the streets.

As we celebrate St. Mark today, I want us to reflect on three things:

I.   *Mark followed the Apostles closely and he became an evangelist.*

Who do you mingle with and what are you learning from them? How are you shaped by the company you keep?

II.   St. Mark left us a Gospel account.

What is your impact on this generation? What will you leave behind for generations to come? What good can people associate with you?

III.   St. Mark took the Good News of Jesus to Alexandria, where he eventually died. He bore fruit in Alexandria.

He fulfilled in his own way the mandate of Jesus as we have it in today's Gospel, *go out to the whole world; proclaim the Good News to all creation....*

We may also ask ourselves: Am I bearing fruit? Where am I witnessing? When He calls me to render account of my stewardship, how many more talents will I be able to present to him? Who have I taken Jesus to or taken to Jesus? How many souls have known the way through me?

St. Catherine of Siena, Virgin & Doctor

Memorial

———— ❦❦❦ ————

READING TEXTS: *1 John 1:5-2:2; Psalm 103; Matthew 11:25-30*

In today's First reading, St. John talked about living in darkness and living in light. What does it mean to live in darkness?

This morning, I will just highlight five points:

I.   To live without understanding of God, and knowledge of His will, is to live in darkness.

II.   Living without joy is to live in darkness. A world of sadness, regret, despair and depression is a dark world.

III. To live in darkness is to live without love for others - a life of hatred and unforgiveness.

IV.   To live without a good relationship with Christ, who is the light of the world is darkness (John 1:9, 8:12).

V.   To be comfortable in habitual sin, is to exist in darkness.

Today, Jesus the Light of the world says, *come to me.* He is willing to shed His clear light on us and liberate us from the dominion of darkness   us, His children of light.

An example of a child of light is St. Catherine of Siena, whom we celebrate today.

St. Catherine of Siena was born in Siena in 1347. Jesus appeared to her when she was six years old. She

61

dedicated herself to God at the age of 7. She refused all arrangements to make her marry the husband of her late sister Bonaventura. After many prayers, much fasting and divine intervention, she was allowed to join the tertiary of the Dominican order. She lived a life of prayer, fasting and abstinence.

In 1370, she was commanded by a vision , to leave her secluded life and enter the public life of the world. She burned with the love of God and her neighbour, dedicating herself to active service for the poor, sick and aged.

She worked assiduously for the reform of clergies, and for the restoration of the seat of the Papacy from France to Rome. She advocated for the supremacy, rights and liberty of the supreme Pontiff, and she worked for peace and harmony among Italian states and between other cities.

St. Catherine of Siena is remembered not just for her piety, stigmata, charity and spiritual writings, but for her political boldness and willingness to 'speak the truth to power'. She died aged 33 on the 29th April 1380 in Rome, eight days after having a stroke.

In 1970 Pope Paul VI declared her a Doctor of the Church, because of her inspiring, orthodox and spiritually nourishing writing. Her body was found incorrupt, 50 years after her death. She was also proclaimed one of the patron saints of Europe, in 1999 by Pope John Paul II.

Through her intercession, may God make us also children of light and vessels of grace in our own time. **Amen.**

Our Lady, Mother of Africa
Feast in Africa
———— ᴇᴄ ᴇᴄ ᴇᴄ ————

READING TEXTS: *Acts 1: 12-14; Resp:Luke 1: 46-55; John 2:1-11*

Today, the Holy Mother Church celebrates the feast of our Lady, Mother of Africa.

This feast is celebrated with special, proper liturgical prayers, set aside to pray that our Lady's intercession may obtain peace, prosperity, faith and vitality for the Church in Africa.

It also prepares us to enter properly into May, the month of our Mother Mary. I strongly believe that Mary has an ardent affection for Africa, and she will not forget her. Africa (precisely Egypt) was the land that sheltered the Holy Family from Herod's violence. The only man who helped Jesus to bear His cross in His time of bitter suffering was Simon from Cyrene, a city currently in Libya.

Today's feast therefore invites us to do at least 3 things.

I.   To pray today for our continent, Africa. The African continent is facing a whole cascade of challenges; economic recession, security problems, civil unrest, ethnic cleansing, threat to peace, religious syncretism, political instability, deep-rooted corruption, educational challenges, moral decadence, Islamic infiltration and domination of hitherto Christian countries, natural disasters.

Our continent needs prayers and today has been set aside to offer prayers for her. Just as our Lady showed the Rosary to St Dominic De Guzman as a weapon for conquering the Albigensians, let us collectively pray the Rosary today for divine intervention in Africa.

II.   Today's feast should also awaken our devotion to our Mother Mary. One of the agendas of the devil is that Mary should be forgotten, so that a major channel of grace to souls be neglected. Devotion to our Mother Mary is one of the unique identities of Catholics; let us not allow this to be taken away from us. Let us renew our love and devotion to her by daily recitation of the rosary, having her picture or statues in our homes, reciting the Magnificat, we fly to your patronage, the Memorare, singing her hymns and a meditative recitation of the Hail Mary and other prayers for her intercession.

Let us always remember to have recourse to her help, not only when the wine is getting exhausted or when it is exhausted, but also when the wine is in good measure. She is a sure help for those who find in her a sure refuge as we have in today's Gospel.

III.   Let us contribute our quarter to building a just, peaceful and great continent. This project starts with "the self". Build your self; embrace values that facilitate development; let your principles be heroic; do your best wherever you find yourself; do not compromise when it means sacrificing truth, justice, decency and other virtues. Let parents make their homes the kind of continent that is admirable (the kind they wish to see Africa become) and build their children to be the kind of leaders that can change the face of this continent.

Let us pray

Loving father, bless us, the people of Africa and the world. Help us to live in justice, love and peace, Mary, Mother of Africa and the world, pray for us.

St. Philip and St. James, Apostles

Feast

READING TEXTS:
1 Corinthians 15:1-8; Psalm 18; John 14:6-14

Today, we celebrate the memorial of Saint Philip and Saint James. Most of what we know about them is what is recorded in the Bible.

Jesus called Philip in Galilee. Philip called Nathaniel (John 1:43-46). Philip was also with Jesus at the multiplication of the loaves (John 6:7). At the Last Supper, Philip was the one who told Jesus to show them the Father (John 14:9 - today's Gospel). He, together with Andrew brought some Greeks to see Jesus (John 12: 20-21).

According to extra-biblical accounts, Philip took the Gospel to Greece, Syria and Phrygia. We are told he converted the wife of the proconsul of the city of Hierapolis, through his miraculous healing and preaching. Out of fury, the proconsul had him crucified upside down and from this cross, he was preaching to the people around him and he converted many.

St. James is called 'the Less' to differentiate him from James the Great, the brother of John and the son of Zebedee. Nothing much is known about him except that he was the Son of Alphaeus. He was also the leader of the Church in Jerusalem. Together with Peter and John, he is called a pillar of the Church (Acts 15:13-21, Galatians 2:9). He is the author of the Epistle of James, which is rich in theology. For instance, we have the exposition on the sacrament of anointing of the sick, the dialectics of faith and work and taming the tongue, a treatise on partiality. James also died a martyr's death at the close of the Passover in the year 62AD, in Jerusalem, during the reign of Nero.

He was asked to deny Jesus publicly, but instead he preached about Him and testified to His resurrection. In his preaching, he converted many who came for the Passover. In fury, the Jewish leaders had him thrown from the top of the temple. He fell and was badly injured but did not die. He was stoned severely and severally until someone issued a blow with his club and he expired.

What is extraordinary about these Saints?

I.   They were followers of Jesus
II.   They were faithful to Him to the end - only extraordinary men could do that.
III. They were His witnesses in the world.
IV.   They loved Christ more than their lives; they laid down their lives for what they believed.
V.   They are now in heaven (not a place for uncommitted Christians).

These 5 things are also important in the making of a Christian:

1.   To be associated with Jesus.
2.   Faithfulness to Jesus to the end.
3.   Witnessing to Jesus by a life of charity.
4.   To love Christ more than our lives.
5.   To live in this world with heaven in mind.

Through the intercession of St. James and Philip, may God make us worthy of eternal happiness with Him. **Amen.**

The English Martyrs

Feast in England

READING TEXTS:
Acts 7:55-60; Psalm 31; Matthew 10:17-20

Today the Holy Mother Church celebrates the feast of the English Martyrs.

We celebrate on this day, not only the forty martyrs of England and Wales who were canonized on the 25th October1970 by Pope Paul VI, but also the 242 declared Blessed. In fact, we celebrate so many unknown Catholics who died defending their faith in a period of around 150 years, following the reformation (1535-1679).

Some of them were hanged; some died in prison; some were tortured to death; some of them were disembowelled and some were cut into quarters - what was called being drawn and quartered.

What was their offence?

They remained true to their Catholic faith at a time of violent persecution against Catholics in England and Wales. It began with King Henry VIII declaring himself supreme head of the Church in England and Wales.

These holy men and women laid down their lives to defend the supremacy of the Pope, the unity of the Church, and the Holy Sacrifice of the Mass. For this, they were charged with treason against the state and religion; they were called recusants and were tortured and killed.

67

The martyrs celebrated today came from every walk of life. There were rich and poor; married and single; men and women, priests, religious men and women and lay faithful.

Lessons for us today:

I.   We remember this day, the selfless sacrifice made by so many, that the faith might live in England. They sowed their blood, their tears, their lives so that you and I may reap the harvest of faith. The feast of today challenges us to do our own part in sowing the seed of faith for future generations and to contribute our own quota for the survival and preservation of the faith.

II.   Their example teaches us fortitude.

While many people recanted at the point of death, many others were willing and in fact were joyful to lay down their lives. They endured bitter death because they had hope of eternal life. They trusted in the words of Jesus in Matthew 16:25:

For whoever wants to save their life will lose it, but whoever loses their life for me will find it.

Today, in one way or the other, we face subtle persecutions in our faith too. Sometimes we have to endure mockery, we are treated with suspicion and unfairly judged on account of our Christian faith and values. Let us be strengthened by the heroic example of fortitude of these great men and women.

May their prayers and examples, the example of Stephen in today's First Reading, the words of Jesus in today's Gospel and the continuing sacrifice made by so many in other less tolerant areas of the world today, inspire us to cherish and be faithful to our profession of faith, and be willing to defend, preserve, share and endure any opposition to it.

Our Lady of Fatima

Optional Memorial

PETER'S DEFENCE OF HIS ACTION

READING TEXTS:
Acts 11:1-18; Psalm 42; John 10:1-10

I want us to draw two lessons from today's First Reading and a challenge from the Gospel.

In the First Reading, we read about the reaction of some men who were party to what Peter did. They criticised him for visiting the Gentiles and spreading the Gospel message to them. They had judged his action in their minds even without giving him a fair hearing. The Greek word is 'peritomeis'; that is, they furiously negated his action. They expressed their total intolerance of his deeds. Their Christianity had not taken away their ill feeling towards the Gentiles.

It is the same with some of us; when our daily Masses, our catalogue of devotions and piety have not taken away our hatred for people and our ill manners (this is an issue for another day). However, Peter calmly explained why he did what he did. He was prompted by God; although his action might have been culturally inexplicable, it was a divine initiative.

I.   Let us be slow to criticise; it is a mortal sin to criticise someone without a fair hearing or thorough investigation. We need to first ascertain that someone did what he/she is accused of and we must also make effort to find out why.

II. Peter was not hurt or angry; he didn't flare up or lose his patience. Though he had the authority of a supreme leader, he calmly endured the torrents of criticism and when they stopped, we are told he explained them in order. He was orderly because he was not furious.

A sure indication of affective maturity is our disposition to criticism and our attitude to correction. This is what many of our leaders, especially in the Church, need to learn. Some feel that to correct them means that you do not appreciate their efforts; to criticise them is conspiracy; to subject their initiative to rational scrutiny means you are frustrating them.

We must learn from Peter to be well disposed to the negation of our submission; whether this negation is done in good faith or otherwise is not the immediate issue. We must be prepared enough to calmly define and defend our stance or, better still, we must have a stance that we can defend without appealing to force, threat, emotion or insult.

III. In today's Gospel, Jesus delineates the defining ingredient of a good shepherd: sacrifice. He makes sacrifices for His flock. The word here is 'laying down'. He gives up, He lets go, He takes their place in suffering. He presents Himself in their stead to prevent them from suffering. This model is clearly lacking today; we usually love ourselves more than those in our care. A leader who is more interested in him/herself than the flock is a 'mercenarium autem' - a hired and self-seeking shepherd, unworthy of the office of shepherding.

So, the question arises, Where do we belong?

Our Lady of Fátima

Today the church commemorates the visions of Our Lady, seen near Fátima in Portugal in 1917, by three shepherd children, Lúcia dos Santos and her cousins Jacinta and Francisco Marto. The visions occurred on the 13th day of each month from May to October, and by October huge crowds were gathering at the site of the visions and reporting further visions and miraculous occurrences themselves.

Pope John Paul II was devoted to Our Lady of Fátima and attributed his survival of an assassin's bullet on 13 May 1981 to her intervention. Jacinta and Francisco Marto, who died in the great Spanish Flu pandemic of 1919-20, were beatified on 13 May 2000. Through the intercession of our Lady of Fátima, may God help us to live out the Christian life.

St. Matthias, Apostle

Feast

READING TEXTS:
Acts 1:15-17, 20-26; Psalm 113; John 15:9-17

Today dear friends we celebrate the Feast of St. Matthias. Matthias, just like Matthew, means 'gift of Yahweh'.

Matthias was the disciple chosen to replace Judas. The First Reading of today narrates how he was selected. Peter presided over the assembly; he gave the address and they nominated Justus and Matthias. They prayed and the lot fell on Matthias and he was enrolled with the eleven apostles.

Matthias had been with Jesus from the baptism of John. He enjoyed good times with the Lord and also endured many hardships with Him. He didn't turn back when many did. He stayed 'til he was eventually chosen to replace Judas.

According to tradition, he took the Gospel first to Cappadocia and later to the Barbarians and Cannibals in Ethiopia. He was stoned to death at Colchin and buried there, near the temple of the sun in 80AD.

We can learn two lessons from today's Feast.

I. *Judas lost his place*

Like Judas we are all called by God to be useful to Him. As we hear in today's Gospel, Jesus calls us as His friends; He calls us out of love, to remain in His love and to bear lasting fruits.

72

We have a responsibility to remain in His love by keeping His commandments. Let us be careful not to lose this privilege. Let us be careful not to lose the love and grace of God (1 Corinthians 10:12).

II.   *No one is indispensable*

Judas was very important in the apostolic college; he was even the treasurer. Yet when he proved himself unworthy, when he chose not to follow the voice of the shepherd and he went astray, another person took his place. In things of God, it is God who makes one worthy, but God can't be dependent on anyone. God can't be held to ransom. For anyone who chooses to be unworthy, God will always prepare a worthier person, as also in the case of Saul and David.

This should teach us humility, carefulness and vigilance.

The Ascension of the Lord

Solemnity

—⚮⚮⚮—

READING TEXTS:
Acts 1:1-11; Psalm 47; Ephesians 1:17-23; Luke 24:46-53

Every 25th December, Christians (particularly) celebrate the Birth of Christ - the day He came into the world. Today, we celebrate the end of Jesus' earthly ministry; the day He left this world. His departure didn't end in death the way every body's earthly journey ends, but in a glorious ascension into heaven. The story of Jesus began with condescension and ended in Ascension, began with incarnation and ended with exaltation.

Today, let us reflect on the meaning and message of the Ascension.

I. The bodily Ascension of Jesus is heaven's affirmation that Jesus had accomplished everything He had to do. It was like 'a welcome' by the Father and a 'send forth' by the Apostles - the end of His physical existence. It was a celebration of Christ's final victory, on account of which the Father raised Him up into glory.

II. By the Ascension, Jesus was going to prepare a place for us as He promised (John 14). As such, we should live in expectation and anxiety of being with the Lord, because where our treasure is, there our hearts ought to be (Matthew 6:21).

III. The Ascension marks the beginning of the ministry of the disciples. Jesus had handed over the baton to them. They now had to carry on what He had commanded them to do. We are the disciples of today. Today's feast reminds us that we have received the mandate to continue the ministry of Jesus.

IV. The Ascension of Jesus marks the start of His high priestly work. He now lives to intercede for us (Hebrews 7:25). He is our advocate before the Father; a sympathetic and merciful High Priest. This should inspire confidence in us that we have someone in not just a high place, but in the highest place always pleading our cause before God.

V. The Ascension marks the official beginning of the disciples' preparation for the coming of the promised Holy Spirit (Act 16:7) and the preparation for Christ's second coming. So, it is also for us to begin a special prayer for a renewed experience of the power of the Holy Spirit at Pentecost.

As we reflect on this significant event, let us ponder on this:

There is a time for everything (Ecclesiastes 3:1).

Jesus was once with the disciples; death took Him for some time. He rose again and stayed with them awhile. From today, after He ascended, they were no longer able see Him physically among them. The Ascension marked the end of His physical presence with them. He was with them for a while and now He was no longer with them physically; any opportunity they had missed was missed forever.

There is also time allotted to all matters under earth; there is a time to repent, a time to do penance, a time to reconcile, a time to do good, a time to cherish one another. We don't have forever to be friends, families, to be classmates or colleagues, to work in a parish or hold an office. Whatever good you ought to do, do it while you have time. Whoever you need to appreciate, appreciate before your time or their time elapses. Whatever good you need to do, do it quickly; time and opportunities wait no longer. They are irretrievable and are always moving.

Lord Jesus, when our earthly journey comes to an end, may we rise again to be with you where you are seated at the Father's right side.
Amen.

St. Augustine of Canterbury

Feast (for the Church in England and Wales)

AMBASSADORS OF THE LORD

READING TEXTS:
1 Thessalonians 2:2-8; Psalm 117; Luke 10:1-9

In the First Reading of today, St. Paul defended the motivation behind his pastoral ministry among the Thessalonians.

His points he made are:

- The ministry was entrusted to him by God.
- His interest was never to deceive, to create impression, to please people, to seek honour or for material gains.
- His motivation was obedience to God who has entrusted him with the ministry and a genuine love of the people among whom he ministered.

In the Gospel of today, we have the account of Jesus sending out seventy-two others ahead of him to share in His mission. In the specific instructions He gave them, three points are very vivid:

I.   They must trust absolutely in God for success and sustenance.
II.   They must not be distracted by social interactions or material gains but must remain focused on the assignments they were given.
III. Wherever they went, they must be agents of peace,

ministers of God's power and ambassadors of the news of God's kingdom.

What is God teaching us through these points?

Like Paul and like the seventy-two messengers, we are also ambassadors of Christ and His kingdom in the world.

Three points for us to ponder on as ambassadors;

1. In everything we do in life, our motivation must be obedience and love of God and love for people.
2. We must look up to God and trust Him for success, sustenance and help. He has all that we need, and He is a faithful God.
3. We must always be agents of peace, ministers of God's power and bearers of good news.

St. Augustine of Canterbury

Today we celebrate in England, the life of St. Augustine of Canterbury.

He was a Prior to the monastery of St. Andrew in Rome. Pope Gregory chose him to be among the missionaries sent to South Eastern England in 596. He responded in gracious obedience.

Augustine faced lots of difficulties, but he endured with patience, trusting in God's plan, goodness and support. He eventually became the first Bishop of Canterbury and he established two more Sees at London and Rochester in Kent. He organised the Church in England and gained so many souls for God by his example of holiness, his love for the people and his words of preaching. He died in Canterbury on 26th May, 605.

May His examples and prayers help us to be true ambassadors of Jesus Christ in our own age and time.
Amen.

The Visitation of Blessed Virgin Mary

Feast

READING TEXTS:
Zephaniah 3:14-18; (Resp) Isaiah 12; Luke 1:39-56

Today, the Holy Mother Church celebrates the feast of the Visitation of the Blessed Virgin Mary to her kinsman Elizabeth. We reflect on this event each time we pray the joyful mysteries of the Holy Rosary. It is also a very wonderful way to end the May devotion, by reflecting on her charity and complete selflessness.

Today, let us ponder these two points:

I.   The selflessness of Mary

It seems more natural to us to desire to be served. We want people to help us, pay attention to our needs, to be supportive to us. We are reluctant to make sacrifices for others, but we want people to make sacrifices for us.

Today, the example of Mary can inspire us. She was in a state of uncertainty and anxiety, a state where she should desire all attention and assistance. She transcended the limitation of self-absorption; she was still willing to go and render help to her kinswoman, prompted by genuine charity and true concern for others.

At some point, we must start looking less into ourselves, shift the focus from ourselves as the centre of attention, to seeing how we can also reach out to others in their need.

79

II.   True devotion is inspired by the Holy Spirit

Upon seeing Mary, Elizabeth was filled by the Holy Spirit and she immediately became prophetic. In that prophetic state, she proclaimed Mary as Blessed, the Mother of my Lord, the most Blessed among all women.

This establishes the connection between true devotion to Mary and the Holy Spirit. No one can recognise the sanctity and dignity of our Blessed Mother, except if prompted by the Holy Spirit, and it is the same Holy Spirit that inspires true devotion to her.

Anyone who finds devotion to the Mother of the Lord regardless of his/her status, whether idolatrous or condemnable, such a person is undoubtedly under the influence of a Spirit that is from our Holy God. Love for the Blessed Mother is a sign that the Holy Spirit is present and is at work in a soul.

As we celebrate the Visitation of the Blessed Virgin Mary to her kinswoman, may we rejoice to receive, through her intercession, the joy that the Holy Spirit gives and the virtue of charity and complete selflessness.

Pentecost Sunday

Solemnity

READING TEXTS: *Acts 2:1-11; Psalm 104; 1 Corinthians 12:3-7,12-13; John 20:19-23*

Dearly beloved in the Lord, today the Holy Mother Church celebrates the feast of Pentecost. Pentecost is from the Greek word (Πεντηκοστή) pentēcostēs, and in Hebrew it is ' שבועות *Shavuot'*. It means fiftieth.   It is also called the Festival of the Weeks. Pentecost is celebrated 7 weeks/50days after the Passover.

Pentecost is an agricultural feast and the first fruits of the wheat harvest were celebrated on this same day (Exodus 23:16, Leviticus 23:15-22). The people brought in their first fruits in gratitude to God.

Later, after the destruction of the temple in 70 AD, the Jews celebrated on this day, the giving of the law to Moses on Mount Sinai.

The wisdom of God

On this day of Pentecost, God chose to give to humanity the first fruit of Christ's Death and Resurrection; that is the Holy Spirit. He gave humanity something more than the Law. He gave us the Holy Spirit, who teaches us to know the will of God and empowers us to do it.

The Lord chose today to fulfil His promise of sending us a paraclete, a counsellor, a teacher, a helper, a comforter. Today, therefore, marks the birthday of the Church. On this day, may we reflect on the work of the

81

Holy Spirit in our lives.

The Holy Spirit in the life of a Christian

I will identify five ways of identifying the Holy Spirit in our lives and preach on one.

I.   A TEACHER:
     The Holy Spirit bestows intellectual virtues of wisdom, knowledge and understanding. He teaches and enlightens us on the ways and things of God (1 Corinthians 2:10-13).

II. A HELPER:
     The Holy Spirit helps us to live out the Christian life and virtues (Romans 8:8).

III. A GIVER:
     The Holy Spirit bestows gifts on souls; different gifts for the building of the Body of Christ. This can be seen in the Second Reading of today (also read 1 Corinthians 12:4-11, 28-31; Romans 12:6-8).

IV. A COUNSELLOR:
     The Holy Spirit is given to us to direct our paths, instruct us, warn us, prompt us. We see how the Holy Spirit directed the life, ministry and missionary endeavour of the early Church in the Acts of the Apostles.

V.   A COMFORTER:
     This is very important, and this is what I want to reflect on today. The Holy Spirit is a great comforter.

Often, we go through life hurt, broken, distressed and sometimes depressed. The Holy Spirit could be our friend, to comfort us, if only we would open ourselves and develop a relationship with Him and invite Him into our lives.

He comforts us either by strengthening us, or by liberation. He strengthens us to boldly face our challenges. He also heals and liberates us from anxiety, fear, depression, frustration, the agony of loneliness, bitterness and unforgiveness, anger of the soul, brokenness, addictions, panic attacks, from a disordered life, from an obstinate spirit of guilt.

Today is a great opportunity for us to experience the healing, liberation and transformation that the Holy Spirit gives.

Let us ask the Spirit of God to come into our hearts and restore order as He did at creation, to dispel fear and anxiety as He did for the Apostles. Let us pray for the peace of the Holy Spirit.
Amen.

St. Charles Lwanga & Companions, Martyr

Memorial

COURAGE AND FORTITUDE
FROM THE HOLY SPIRIT

READING TEXTS:
Those applicable for the day

In many parts of Africa, today is observed as a feast day in honour of St. Charles Lwanga, an example of someone in whose life we can see the manifestation of courage and fortitude. St. Charles Lwanga is the patron saint of African Catholic Youth Action.

St. Charles was a Ugandan convert to the Catholic faith. King Mwanga II of Uganda, in a bid to resist foreign colonisation, charged that Christian converts should abandon their faith; he even massacred many Anglican missionaries.

Joseph Mukassa, the head of the royal court's attendants, reproached the king for this and was beheaded. Lwanga then took the place of Mukassa. However, Lwanga, after being baptised, was secretly teaching other court attendants' catechism and was baptising them. He incurred the wrath of the king, most particularly because he was discouraging the youths at the palace from participating in sexual acts with the king.

He was rounded up with other Christians in the royal court. Some of them were speared, but Lwanga and his companions were tortured and then burnt alive.

On June 3, 1886, Charles Lwanga was separated from the others and burned at the stake. The executioners slowly burnt his feet until only the charred remains were left. Still alive, they promised him that they would let him go if he renounced his faith. He refused saying, Y ou are burning me, but it is as if you are pouring water over my body.   He then continued to pray silently as they set him on fire. Just before the flames reached his heart, he looked up and said in a loud voice, Katonda!   My God! and died.

His companions were all burned together the same day, all the while praying, and singing hymns until they died.

There were 24 protomartyrs in all. The last of the protomartyrs, a young man named John Mary, was beheaded by King Mwanga on January 27, 1887.

The persecutions spread during the reign of Mwanga, with 100 Christians, both Catholics and Protestants, being tortured and killed.

St. Charles and many other martyrs for the faith died between November 15, 1885 and January 27, 1887 in Namugongo, Uganda.

St. Charles and his companions were beatified in 1920 and canonised by Pope Paul VI in 1964.

As we reflect today on the life of St. Charles Lwanga, let us also consider these three messages:

I.   *Obedience and loyalty to God come before obedience to any human authority.*

In Acts 5:29, Peter and the other disciples reaffirmed this message. We must obey God before any human being.

II.   Our faith must be practised no matter the circumstances.

St. Charles was in an unfavourable situation, yet it was not an excuse for him to abandon or jettison his faith. This reminds us of the story of Daniel. Even when the king had issued a decree that no one should pray to any other god except him, Daniel continued his practice of faith. He was arrested but God chose to deliver him (Daniel 6).

III.   It is cowardice, compromise, betrayal of the Lord and conspiracy for a Christian to be comfortable in a situation of injustice, immorality and corruption.

Charles could not be silent on the corruption orchestrated by the king; he sought ways to put an end to it and that attracted the wrath of the king. But again, what does it matter? It is better to attract the wrath of an earthly king and gain the friendship and commendation of the King of kings.

Though St. Charles was tortured and murdered for his faith and constancy, his witness and love of God, he now lives with God for ever. Those who lose their lives for love of God never die, for they are alive with God forever.

Through the prayers of St Charles Lwanga, may God grant us courage to witness and fortitude to remain faithful to the Lord, especially when it is strangely too difficult.

May the martyrs of Uganda, pray for Christians who are suffering because of their faith, that God may give them courage, zeal, and joy. May God also help those of us who live in places where Christianity is accepted, to remain aware of the persecution in other parts of the world.
Amen.

The Most Holy Trinity

Solemnity

READING TEXTS: *Proverbs 8:22-31; Psalm 8; Romans 5:1-5, John 16:12-15*

Today is the first Sunday after Pentecost. Having experienced the power of the Holy Spirit anew and the understanding He gives, the Church wants us to reflect on the most fundamental mystery of our faith - the mystery of the Trinity; the mystery of God's inner life.

The Trinity

Our God is a community of three persons, who are co-eternal in existence, co-equal in power, glory and divinity, and co-substantial in essence. They are undivided in unity; they exist in a communion of love and in function. Although they are distinct, they do not operate in isolation.

In them, there is no conflict, suspicion, disunity or disharmony.

The immediate message

God revealed His inner life to us in order to be a model for all human relationships. This model is very important as even now conflict and mutual suspicion have ruined many families, Churches and communities of friends. Our project is to seek ways to build our relationships around this model and seek to repair disintegrated relationships to reflect that of the Trinity.

A deeper reflection on the Trinity

One day, Thales (an Ancient Greek Philosopher)

was pondering on the wonder of the skies and he fell into a pit. A young girl seeing him made fun of him saying that he should pay closer attention to what was around him, before considering what was above him.

As we seek to ponder on God's inner life in Himself, God is also inviting us to ponder on our own lives as well - a journey of self-awareness.

Self-awareness
This hinges on two points:

I.   Understanding the power, glory and grace God has deposited in each of us.

Many people today feel so worthless, angry with themselves and others, and envious of others and therefore live in self-pity, because they lack knowledge of what God has planted in them. The Psalmist of today says, *yet   you have made him little less than a god; with glory and honour you crowned him.*

Read 1 Samuel 17: not everyone believed in David, yet he knew himself and believed in the grace he had received. He conquered Goliath to the amazement of everyone. This is called self-awareness.

II.   Understanding our weaknesses and the harm/pains we cause to others.

Often, we are blind to our faults; we see what is wrong with every other person. We become proud, we blame, judge, complain and condemn others for weaknesses that overflow in us. We listen to reflections, but we do not see ourselves in the picture. We cause others so much harm and pain and yet we feel normal.

We feel complete, whereas we are full of negative traits like the Church in Laodicea (Revelation 3:17).

Often, we are unaware of our blind spots and it becomes difficult for us to grow to become better. Many are those living in the illusion of righteousness and holiness, whereas in reality, they are miles away from it.

How do I discover myself?

In today's Gospel Jesus said: when the Spirit of truth comes, He will lead you to the complete truth. The greatest truth is the truth about oneself, and it is a journey. It is in fact the farthest journey in which only the Holy Spirit can lead us (1 Corinthians 2:11); the journey to the self where He will reveal the truth about the self to the self. Often, the revelation is very shocking.

May we ask the Holy Spirit to lead us to the truth about ourselves; the truth that will enable us to understand God better, to grow in Christian maturity and peace, which will help us to relate more peacefully with others.

The Body and Blood of Christ *(Corpus Christi)*

Solemnity

READING TEXTS: *Genesis 14:18-20; Psalm 110; 1 Corinthians 11:23-26; Luke 9:11-17*

Last week, we celebrated the most fundamental mystery of the Christian faith - the mystery of the Trinity. Today, we are also celebrating the solemnity of the greatest gift of Jesus to the Church; the centre of all else the Church has and does. We are celebrating the solemnity of the Body and Blood of Jesus.

Three dimensions to today's celebration

I.   We want to thank the Lord for giving us the Sacrament of His Body and Blood. While the other sacraments give grace, the Holy Eucharist gives Jesus Himself, the author of all graces.

II.   We shall reflect on the meaning and purpose of the Holy Eucharist.

III.   We shall make reparations and ask for mercy for every unworthy reception of Holy Communion and every sin of sacrilege, irreverence, neglect, indifference and doubt committed against Jesus, present among us in this sublime sacrament and in the tabernacles all over the world.

Why did Jesus give us Himself?

Let's just examine these three reasons:

I.   Jesus gave us His Body and Blood as a pledge, sign and evidence of His presence with us (Matthew

28:20). Jesus is not just in heaven, He is here. Im-
anu-el means present in the Holy Eucharist. He is
with us in the Blessed Sacrament and He comes to
us and mixes with our spiritual DNA when we
receive Him in Holy Communion. What a mystery!
To think of Jesus giving Himself to us as humble
food.

II.   Jesus gave us the Eucharist as a reminder of His
        sacrifice and as a reassurance of His love for us.
        Pope Francis calls it a memorial of God's love
        (Homily on Corpus Christi, June 18, 2017 at the
        square of the Basilica of St John Lateran, Rome).

III.   Jesus has given Himself to us in the Holy Eucharist
        as a powerful means of grace; grace of healing,
        strength, comfort, peace and strengthening of
        divine life in us.

Message

I.   A call for penance

As we thank the Lord today, may we also keep in
mind the messages of the Blessed Virgin Mary in her
numerous apparitions. She complains so bitterly about
the sins we commit against the sublime sacrament of
love, especially sins of sacrilegious communion, doubts
and irreverence.

Let us today be truly repentant and do penance.

II.   Becoming the Eucharist

The readings of today talk about offering. Abram
offered gifts to Melchizedek; Jesus offered bread to the
hungry multitude, an offering He perfected by offering
Himself. As we also receive Jesus the Bread of Life, let
us keep in mind that the Eucharist challenges us to offer
ourselves for others too. We are to become the Eucharist
- bread broken for others. We have before us the

example of St. Paul who said: *my   life has been poured out as a libation* (2 Timothy 4:6). This week we had the example of St. Alban and Aloysius Gonzaga.

Whenever we offer ourselves for others, we become like Jesus in the Eucharist; we become bread broken for others.

The Most Sacred Heart of Jesus

Solemnity

READING TEXTS:
Ezekiel 34:11-16; Psalm 23; Romans 5:5-11; Luke 15:3-7

Today, the Holy Mother Church celebrates the Solemnity of the Sacred Heart of Jesus. On the 16th June 1675, our Blessed Lord appeared to St. Margaret Mary Alacoque, revealing His Sacred Heart and requesting the establishment of the feast on the Friday after Corpus Christi. We are to make reparations for sins which offend His Sacred Heart especially the sins of irreverence, indifference, sacrilege committed against Jesus in the Holy Eucharist, as well as the sins of ingratitude of humanity for the sacrifice that He made for us.

On Sunday, we reflected on the body and blood of Jesus, the supreme gift of love to humankind, and we made reference to these sins.

Today, may we turn our gaze to the Sacred Heart of our Lord Jesus Christ, a heart full of incomprehensible love for all humanity; a merciful heart full of compassion, a gentle heart. It is also a heart that grieves for the sins of humanity; sins of man's inhumanity to man, sins of hypocrisy, rejection of divine love, obstinacy in sin; not just sins of some unidentified humanity but my own sins.

Today's feast invites us to both celebration and contrition.

94

We celebrate the fact that the heart of Jesus beats with love of us. That Jesus loves me is big news. I cannot get used to it; it does not stop amazing me: that He is not thinking of punishing me but forgiving me. He wants to pamper me and enfold me in His arms like a loving shepherd would tenderly enfold his weak lamb. This thought makes me want to cry.

Today is also a day of contrition, to ask God for mercy for the many times we have wounded the Sacred Heart by our doubts, disobedience, refusal to trust in the love of Jesus, impurity, lack of charity to others and all the sins committed against Jesus in the Most Holy Sacrament of the Altar. We want to tell Jesus how sorry we are.

Today, let us pray:
I love you Jesus, my love, above all things: I repent with my whole heart of having offended you. Never permit me to separate myself from you again. Grant that I may love you always; and then do with me what you will.

Sacred Heart of Jesus... Your kingdom come.

The Immaculate Heart of the Blessed Virgin Mary

Memorial

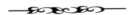

READING TEXTS:
2 Chronicles 24:17-25; Psalm 89:4-5, 29-34; Luke 2:41-51

Yesterday, we celebrated the Solemnity of the Sacred Heart of Jesus. Today, we turn to the Blessed Virgin Mother and celebrate her Immaculate Heart. This is not surprising because Mother and Son live in an inseparable union of love.

What do we mean by the Immaculate Heart of Mary?

We mean that the heart of Mary is pure, chaste, sinless and stainless. This is largely part of the grace she enjoyed as the Mother of God the Son and also by her own effort to keep her heart pure.

What is a pure heart?

Let's look at four qualities of a pure and immaculate heart.

I.   A pure heart is a heart that doesn't allow sinful thoughts, imagination and desire to rest in it. It is a heart that doesn't willfully accommodate sinful desires and thoughts.

II. A pure heart is a heart that nurses no envy, bitterness or hatred for anyone. A heart that accommodates hatred or envy is a heart that is defiled and damaged.

III. A pure heart is a heart that ponders on the Word of God and allows it to dwell therein, just as Mary did in today's Gospel. This is also what the Gospel acclamation proclaims.

IV.   A pure heart is a heart that occupies itself with holy and sublime thoughts; thoughts of God, of heaven, of eternal life, of virtues; a heart that contemplates the holiness and awesomeness of God.

Matthew 5:8 tells us that only those with this kind of heart will see God.

As we celebrate the Immaculate Heart of Mary, we are being invited to examine the state of our own hearts. Are they pure or striving for purity, or do we have a heart completely stained with sin?

Psalm 24:3-4, *who   shall ascend the hill of the Lord? And who shall stand in His holy place? Those who have clean hands and pure hearts, who do not lift up their souls to what is false...*

Dear friends, people may be interested in how we look, but God is, in contrast, interested in the state of our hearts (2 Samuel 16:7). Let us each make our heart a suitable temple where God can dwell, so that we can also become suitable to dwell in the temple of God in eternity.

The Nativity of St. John the Baptist

Solemnity

READING TEXTS:
Isaiah 49:1-6; Psalm 139; Acts 13:22-26; Luke 1:57-66, 80

Today, the Church celebrates the Nativity of St. John the Baptist. The circumstances surrounding the birth of John, his identity and mission are so significant that the church found it imperative to celebrate his birth.

As we know, the Church celebrates the day a saint passes from this world; that is the day they are reborn into a glorious eternal destiny. That is their real birthday. However, the Church reserves the celebration of birthdays for three people:

I.   St. John the Baptist, who was sanctified, consecrated and commissioned in the womb.

II. Our Mother Mary, who from the very instance of her conception was without the least stain or guilt of sin and was designated to be the mother of the saviour of humanity.

III. Our Lord Jesus Christ, the saviour of humanity, who was human like us in all things but without sin.

Having established this background, let us reflect on three points from today's celebration:

I.   Everyone has a mission. Everyone that God created is created with a mission. No one comes to this world without 'essence'. Every child is a child of purpose. A child is created by God to fulfil a

98

destiny. Every being created has a mission in the world.

In the language of philosophy, our essence precedes existence and not otherwise . The readings of today affirm this:

Isaiah says in the First Reading, *The Lord called me from the womb, from the body of my mother he named my name....*

God defined his mission from the womb as follows, *...you should be my servant to raise up the tribes of Jacob and to restore the preserved of Israel, I will give you as a light to the nations, that my salvation may reach to the end of the earth.* (What a mission!)

The second stanza two of the Psalm today proclaims the same:
For it was you who formed my inmost being, knit me together in my mother's womb.

The Second Reading of today opens and continues this way, *In those days, Paul said, God raised up David to be our Father's king... of this man's posterity God has brought to Israel a Saviour* (This is David's essence and purpose).

The circumstances surrounding the birth of John also re-affirm this truth. He is a child of destiny, mission and purpose. This truth comes with two implications.

i. No child is useless or worthless. No pregnancy is to be willfully terminated because the life terminated is a child of promise and purpose. He/she is an answer to some questions in life, a solution to some situations. In a child is a potential generation of unpredictable mission.

The interesting truth is that often, children with very bright and exceptionally significant missions and unprecedented destinies sometimes come at what might be called the 'wrong' or a 'strange' time. Look at Samuel, Samson, Isaac, John and even Jesus.

ii. All of us must realise that we are in this world for a purpose. The moment we start fulfilling our purpose in life is when we start living. The fundamental purpose of every one of us is to be a blessing to the world, to better the world, to bring joy, sweetness and meaning to the life of others.

More importantly, our greatest purpose is to work out our salvation. We are here on earth to prepare for our eternal salvation.

II. At the birth of John, people asked, what will this child be?. John turned out to be a blessing to humanity. At the birth of every child, the same concern is expressed, what will this child be?

Now, we have reached an age of self-definition, we may want to ask ourselves, what have I turned out to be? Who have I become? Am I an answer/ solution to a problem or a problem to be solved?

III. John was specifically given his name by God. We have several instances in the Bible of God changing people's names by Himself. Let us cite few instances here. God changed:

- Abram to Abraham in Genesis 17:5
- Sarai to Sarah in Genesis 17:15

- Jacob to Israel in Genesis 32:28
- Simon to Peter in John 1:42.

Why? Well, the reason is that the name we bear is significant.

Names carry power and purpose, destiny and grace. This is why the Church has taught us to consider Saints' names for children at their baptism. John, for instance, is from the Greek "Ioannes", which in turn is derived from the Hebrew yochanan , meaning Yahweh is Gracious" and this reflects the mission of John.

We may need to be more careful and reflective in giving names to our children or grandchildren. It is not even out of place to pray before giving or choosing a name for ourselves (for instance in confirmation or adult baptism) and by extension even for our business or companies.

Happy Feast of the Birthday of St. John to us all!

May God watch over all our children and protect all unborn children.

St. Peter and St. Paul, Apostles

Solemnity

READING TEXTS: *Acts 12:1-11; Psalm 34; 2 Timothy 4:6-8, 17-18; Matthew 16:13-19*

Today, the Holy Mother Church celebrates two of her illustrious sons. They are described as princes, and also as pillars of the Church, because of their significant contributions to the spread of the Gospel of Jesus and the growth of the early Church.

In this homily, I won't be talking about their history or background because we all know them. They are not unfamiliar saints.

Let us just reflect on three lessons from their lives.

I.   Their zeal for God

Paul became an ardent Apostle to the Gentiles, Peter an Apostle to the Jews. They travelled through the length and breadth of the then-known world. They contributed immensely to the spread of the Word of God. They preached and lived out the Gospel. They were zealous about Jesus.

The questions before us are: How passionate/zealous am I in spreading and living my faith? What have I contributed or what am I contributing to the growth of the Church of my time? In what way(s) am I building the Body of Christ - the Church?

II.   They loved Jesus more than their lives

As important as life is, Peter and Paul preferred Jesus to their lives. They laid down their lives, instead of

102

laying down their faith. St. Paul already told us that to him life is Christ and death is gain (Philippians 1:21). They eventually gained their lives by losing them. Peter was crucified upside down, but he is now enjoying a happiness that is everlasting. Paul was beheaded but now he enjoys the everlasting Crown of Glory.

Life is important, but Christ is more important. Nothing is more important than our faith in Jesus. For this we should be ready to lay down anything, our lives included.

Nothing should weigh more than, or close to, God in our lives.

III.   They were not discouraged

The two disciples suffered so much. The First Reading narrates the imprisonment of Peter and the miraculous deliverance. St. Paul, in the Second Reading also tells us, *my   life is already being poured away as a libation.*

Dear friends, Peter and Paul suffered so much, but the interesting thing is that they never gave up; they were not discouraged. They were treated like fools, dogs, criminals, mad men, as enemies of God and rebels. They were beaten, abused, misunderstood, but they never gave up.

So many of us are already discouraged in life because of a little challenge, because people misunderstand us and speak ill of us, because no one acknowledges our sweat. We have given up our good resolutions; our determination is not firm enough to surmount our tribulations. We have joined the race of those who shrink back and are lost (Hebrews 10:39).

The truth is that those who are discouraged and abandon what God has given them to do, will end up doing what Satan wants them to do, and end where the devil wants them to end.

May the prayers of St. Peter and St. Paul help us to be zealous about Jesus, help us to work for the growth of the Church without being discouraged, and help us to prefer our salvation to our comfort.

St. Thomas, Apostle

Feast

━━━━━━━

READING TEXTS:
Ephesians 2:19-22; Psalm 117; John 20:24-29

Today, the Holy Mother Church celebrates the feast of St. Thomas the Apostle, popularly known as doubting Thomas because he initially doubted the resurrection.

In real life also, is it not the case that people are more often remembered or described by their mistakes or weaknesses, rather than by their strength or excellence?

However, there are two wonderful things about Thomas that we often tend to forget. He was the first to confess faith in the divinity of Jesus. Also, in John 11:1-16, it was Thomas who encouraged the rest to follow Jesus to Judaea, even if it involved martyrdom. True to his conviction, Thomas took the Good News outside the Roman Empire, journeying as far as the states of Kerala and Tamil Nadu in present day India.

In India, he converted several people, founding what today is known as 'Saint Thomas Christians' or *Mar Thoma Nazranis*. There, he suffered martyrdom; he was pierced with a lance, at the king's command. He is often regarded as the Patron Saint of India.

Two challenges for us today:
I.   Like Thomas, let us take the Good News wherever we go today. Let it be on our lips, let us ponder it in our hearts and witness to it by our actions. There are souls out there for us to introduce to Jesus.
II.   Let us pray for the love and courage of Thomas; a love and courage that prompted him to be willing to follow Jesus even in danger of death.

St. Mary Magdalene

Feast

———❦❧———

READING TEXTS:
Songs 3:1-4ab; Psalm 63; John 20:1-2, 11-18

Today, the Holy Mother Church celebrates the feast of St. Mary Magdalene. Today's celebration was initially a memorial, but the Holy Father Pope Francis, under the impulse of the Holy Spirit, raised the memorial to the dignity of a liturgical feast, recognising the special role of Mary Magdalene as an apostle to the Apostles, and the first person, chosen by God, to witness the resurrection and to proclaim it.

In Luke 8:2-3 we have an insight as to who Mary Magdalene was.

Mary , called Magdalene, from whom seven demons had gone out... and many others... provided for them (for Jesus and the twelve Apostles) out of their resources.

Some described her as a prostitute; the Bible designates her as the woman from whom Jesus cast out seven demons. So, we know that she was a woman with a shameful past but forgiven, sanctified and restored through grace.

After being restored, she became a follower of Jesus. Other women, as well as Mary Magdalene herself, supported Christ and His disciples out of their resources. Her life revolved round Jesus. She is a worthy

106

example of the love of Jesus. She was the first to run to the empty tomb and refused to leave. For Mary, what was life without Jesus? Dead or alive, all she wanted was Jesus.

Three striking points stand out in today's reflection:

I.   *No one is to be condemned, no one is written off. Grace continues to search for souls to repair, restore and send.*

II. *Mary is an example of those who are dedicated to supporting their priests.*

In the light of the heartbreaking news of scandals, many people have become very critical and suspicious of their own ministers. Others, however, retain their love, respect, prayers and support. While some seek fault, others have devoted themselves to praying for priests. Many men and women of good will have given so much support to priests by their generosity and kindness.

There are people who are sensitive to the needs of their ministers and are eager to go the extra mile to help, out of the love they have for Jesus, the Supreme High Priest. They minister to their ministers from their own means. Today is a day to appreciate those men and women of good will and to ask God to bless their love and generosity. They are a type of Mary Magdalene.

III. *The life of Mary has taught us what it means to love.*

Once restored, her life revolved round Jesus. Jesus was her priority; she had no life outside of Jesus. He was her all in all. She followed Him to the Cross; she ran to the tomb before dawn; she waited at the empty tomb and would never return because outside of Jesus she saw only nothingness and emptiness. She died and was buried in her heart with Jesus. She was a martyr of love; no wonder she was chosen to be the first witness of His glorious Resurrection.

This is the kind of love, proclaimed in today's First Reading from the Songs of Solomon, a lover seeks for her beloved and will stop at nothing to find him, because life for her is an empty space without him.

May we pray for this love. A love for God/Jesus that is GAP (Genuine, Absolute and Perfect).

St. James, Apostle

Feast

---❦❦❦---

TRUE GREATNESS

READING TEXTS:
2 Corinthians 4:7-15; Psalm 126; Matthew 20:20-28

Today, the Holy Mother Church celebrates the feast of St. James, the brother of St. John. James and his brother John were sons of Zebedee, called by Jesus from their fishing. In today's Gospel, we have an account of their mother coming to negotiate with Jesus, to reserve seats of honour for her sons in the cabinet of His government/kingdom.

Jesus asked if they could drink the cup He would drink, and they replied in the affirmative. Eventually, James became the first Apostle to drink the chalice of martyrdom. Herod Agrippa singled him out to be beheaded, not just because he was a leader in the church in Jerusalem, but because of his exceptional zeal.

Today, let us reflect on Jesus' teaching on true greatness in today's Gospel and relate it to St. James.

True greatness

The other disciples were angry with James and John. They knew the importance of power and were equally interested. Jesus used the opportunity to teach them, and indeed all of us, that true greatness does not subsist in being bossy, controlling, commanding, oppressing others or occupying an enviable seat.

109

True greatness consists in three things:

I.   A life of true humility.

Not having a high opinion of oneself, self-awareness of our emptiness, and dependence on God's grace. In the First Reading, St. Paul says we are only earthenware jars. Humility is to be able to tame our ego. Humility is to see less of ourselves, our strength and goodness, and more of God and others.

Greatness is in genuine humility. Being a leader does not automatically amount to being great. Being a leader and yet being humble is greatness (Read Sirach 3:18).

II.   Greatness is not so much in accumulation of power but living a life that inspires and challenges others.

A person is great if his/her life inspires, motivates or challenges others. In this sense we can say St. James was great. His life is an inspiration to us as Christians of today.

III.   True greatness consists in ardent love and zeal for God.

St. James manifested this zeal. He took the Gospel to Spain, before returning to Jerusalem. He was a fearless witness to Jesus; when he had to choose between life and Jesus, he chose Jesus and in choosing Jesus he actually chose eternal life (John 10:10; 14:6).

Greatness is in having zeal for the things of God and in preferring eternal life to long life.

The Transfiguration of the Lord

Feast

———⊱⊰———

READING TEXTS:
Daniel 7:9-10, 13-14; Psalm 97; 2 Peter 1:16-19; Luke 9:28-36

I love the book The Confessions of St. Augustine. It is a book, the contents of which I presume, many people will be able to relate to. It tells the stories of Augustine's struggles, especially his moral and spiritual struggles; how he was addicted to a life of pleasure until he found grace or grace found him.

After he had tasted the sweetness of God, the addictive sweetness of pleasure became vain and unattractive. All he wanted was more of God.

The experience of Augustine is often the experience of those who have tasted the sweetness of knowing God, experiencing His love and glory. The things that once charmed them most, the things they were once addicted to, soon lose all their attractions and fascination. In Philippians 3:7, St. Paul called all he had struggled to gain as inconsequential when compared to the supreme advantage of knowing Jesus.

Today, as we celebrate the transfiguration of the Lord, let us listen to Peter saying: *Master , it is wonderful for us to be here; so, let us make three tents, one for you, one for Moses and one for Elijah.*

He had seen and tasted of the glory of the Lord; he had forgotten about everything else in the world, even

111

his family; all he wanted was to continue to experience this beauty and contemplate this glory. Nothing mattered more than this.

In life, we sometimes get attracted to, and perhaps addicted to, something that gives us pleasure but also troubles our conscience with guilt. We feel helpless.

The truth is that when we taste of true pleasure, true happiness, true joy from God, at once what we feel we cannot do without becomes repulsive and empty of attraction to us. The imperfect dissolves in the face of perfection; the mundane loses value before the divine; the shadow fades before the reality.

Let us pray for this transforming experience, this transfiguration experience; an experience that will liberate us from addiction to worldly pleasure, and make us seek more of God, the one who can truly satisfy us.

St. Lawrence, Deacon & Martyr

Feast

—————

READING TEXTS:
2 Corinthians 9:6-10; Psalm 112; John 12:24-26

Today, the Holy Mother Church celebrates one of her most renowned deacons of antiquity. He is St. Lawrence, born in Oscar, Spain in the year 225 AD. His life and his death are a great lesson for all of us.

In the month of August, in the year 258, the Roman Emperor Valerian issued a decree that all Bishops, Priests and Deacons should be immediately put to death. On the 6th August in the same year, Pope Sixtus together with some Deacons, was apprehended and executed. The Holy Pope was arrested while celebrating Mass and beheaded.

Lawrence too was arrested and since he was in charge of the treasures of the Church, he was instructed to hand over everything to the state. This was requested of Lawrence for three days.

Within the given days, he went to share the treasures of the Church with the poor and the needy. On the fourth day, when he was apprehended and the treasures were requested from him, he brought forward the hungry, the poor, the destitute and presented them to the authorities as the treasures of the Church.

The authorities were furious, and Lawrence was bound and placed on a red-hot burning grid-iron. He accepted this sentence with joy and in the calm assurance that heaven awaited him. In fact, according to some traditions, he was admonishing the executioners to become Christians, lest they suffer a greater punishment. After a while, he managed to tell the executioners, *I am done this side, turn me over.*

As we celebrate the heroic life and death of St. Lawrence, let us reflect on two points:

I.   The poor are very dear to the heart of God. They are the treasures of the Church too and so we must add to our spirituality genuine charity to the poor and needy. Read Proverbs 21:13. Kindness to the poor and needy is one of the quickest routes to access the mercy of God. This is what Lawrence proclaimed eloquently.

II. Life is useless when it is preserved at the expense of faithfulness to God. To be willing to risk our lives to witness to Jesus, is the greatest respect for life. There are times when to choose death is to embrace true life. In this way, Lawrence chose eternal life by choosing death. Every Christian is a potential martyr (2 Corinthians 4:10). Cowardice and witnessing are incompatible. It is at this point we need the grace and courage that the Holy Spirit gives.

The Assumption of the Blessed Virgin Mary

Solemnity

———∞∞∞∞———

READING TEXTS: *Revelation 11:19, 12:1-6, 10; Psalm 45; 1 Corinthians 15:20-26; Luke 1:39-56*

Today, the Holy Mother Church celebrates the solemnity of the Assumption of the Blessed Virgin Mary. This is the Church's testimony to the fact that at the end of Mary's earthly life, she was taken up (assumed) body and soul into heaven and God preserved her from decay.

This has always been taught and believed by the early Church. Many early Saints and defenders of the faith like Ephiphanius of Salamis, Timothy of Jerusalem, Juvena, first Bishop of Jerusalem, Gregory of Tours, John Damascene, John the Theologian, and Germanus of Constantinople preached, taught and wrote extensively on this.

Assumption as a dogma

It was on the 1st November 1950, after much consultation, inspiration and even apparitions, that Pope Pius XII promulgated this as a dogma of faith revealed by God (this promulgation was made in his Apostolic Constitution Munificentissimus Deus).

Assumption prefigured in the Bible

The Bible, especially the Old Testament, already gave us antecedents of those who were assumed body and soul into heaven. They prefigured the assumption of the Blessed Virgin.

115

Elijah for instance, was taken up to heaven body and soul in a whirlwind (cf. 2 Kings 2:1-12).We also have Enoch; according to Genesis 5:24 and Hebrews 11:5, God took Elijah and Enoch to heaven, body and soul.

Message today

Mary surrendered her will in order to embrace God's will. She co-operated to offer herself to God to fulfil His plan for humanity. She served God's purpose with her life and the assumption was part of her reward.

This tells us that it is rewarding to serve the Lord. Like our Blessed Mother Mary, everyone who dedicates his/her life and time to serving the Lord and walking with Him, will be eternally rewarded (Hebrews 6:10).

Sometimes we may think, like the Israelites in Malachi 3:13-18, of what use is it to serve the Lord? Especially when, like Mary, sword-like challenges are piercing our souls too; when the old rugged Cross becomes heavier than we expect, and God seems to be quiet about the whole situation.

This message is an especial encouragement to me, and many other priests who celebrate their priestly anniversary today. It is as well, a message for every Christian that there is a great reward in serving the Lord (working for the Lord) and most particularly, there is great reward in holiness (walking with the Lord).

Like Mary, all who diligently serve the Lord and seek to be pleasing in His sight, will share in the fruit of Christ's redemption, as Mary did.

St. Bartholomew, Apostle

Feast

READING TEXTS:
Revelation 21:9-14; Psalm 145; John 1:45-5

Today, dearly beloved in Christ, the Holy Mother Church celebrates the Feast of St. Bartholomew.

St. Bartholomew was one of the disciples of Jesus. He is also known as Nathaniel. Not much is known about him. The major biblical information we have about him is what we have in today's Gospel. Philip found him and brought him to Jesus and Jesus did his analysis.

According to trustworthy tradition, Bartholomew preached in India. He then travelled from India to Armenia, where he was martyred in Albanopolis. He was flayed alive and crucified upside down because he converted Polymius, the King of Armenia, to Christianity.

What I want to reflect on is Jesus' assessment of Bartholomew. Jesus called him a true Israelite in whom there was no deceit (incapable of deceit). This statement presupposes that we have some Israelites who are adulterated, or if you like - *deceitful*.

Very quickly, let us look at four things that make a true Israelite:

I.   Monotheism: belief in and worship of one God.
II.   A great respect and reverence for the Torah.

III. A living hope and expectation of the Messiah.

IV. Ethnic patriotism.

Jesus 'scanned' Bartholomew and saw him through and through and He saw what no one else could see in Bartholomew. He saw beyond his prejudice to his sincerity and the hidden grace in him.

Two points here:

I. What is there in me for God to see? He is not deceivable and cannot be deluded by pretence. Is there a truth, a sincerity in me or am I a heap of pretence? We are reminded that we are dealing with a God who sees through pretence.

II. No matter my weaknesses and my prejudices, my challenges and circumstances in life, no matter how ugly my story is or how unpleasant my journey has been, God has placed His glory in me. His grace is in my soul and a divine energy is in my depth. He who called Bartholomew also has need of me. He has created me for His purpose and pleasure, so what then will be my excuse?

The Beheading of St. John the Baptist

Memorial

READING TEXTS:
2 Thessalonians 3:6-10, 16-18, Psalm 128, Mark 6:17-29

Today, the Holy Mother Church commemorates the event of the beheading of St. John the Baptist. According to the Gospel, John was beheaded for speaking against injustice, marital infidelity, greed and abuse of power.

Even though Herod beheaded him on earth, that head received the Crown of Glory in heaven and so God has turned this tragedy into a glorious event for us. This is what we celebrate today; the triumph of truth over injustice and wickedness.

Today, I want to call our attention to three things:

I.   Be strong in persecution. St. John was imprisoned not for doing what was wrong, but for speaking the truth. Dear friends in Christ, let us not compromise our faithfulness and courage because we are going through some hard times which are the results of our sincerity and loyalty to Christ. Sometimes those who are supposed to encourage us to stand firm will appeal to our emotion to give up. Dear friends, may I quickly remind you that there is gain in suffering unjustly for the sake of Christ (1 Peter 2:19-21). Read also Matthew 5:10-11.

II. Obedience to our elders, superiors and leaders is very important. However, disobedience is a courageous virtue when it is a response to unjust assignments. Dear friends, we must not allow ourselves to be used by anyone to do evil. We are not bound to obey someone when such obedience implies disobedience to God.

Three people obeyed blindly today and because of this, they are also stained with the blood of John the Baptist.

They are Herod, who obeyed his wife and went on to shed blood; the daughter of Herodias who obeyed her mother; and the soldiers who obeyed a vicious command and beheaded John.

III. Let us also learn to respect human lives. The way people waste the lives of others these days is very disheartening. Dear friends, life is sacred and should be respected. Look at those who have lost their lives to insurgency, in the struggle for political office, for ethnic hegemony, in inter-tribal conflicts.

Let us not walk the path of Herod and his wife. The end for murderers is always tragic and their eternity is inevitably sorrowful.

The Nativity of the Blessed Virgin Mary

Feast

———◦◦◦◦◦———

READING TEXTS:
Micah 5:1-4; Psalm 13; Matthew 1:1-16, 18-23

I was invited to a birthday ceremony recently. The children organised a very grand celebration for their mother for her 70th birthday. During the speeches, the eldest son commented that:

We are so glad to have her as our mother; she is a very loving woman. Without her, we wouldn't be where we are today. She is always praying for us and supporting us. Our only regret is that we can't do more, because nothing is too much for a mother like this (paraphrased).

These touching words resound in my consciousness as today, the Church calls us to celebrate our Mother Mary; a Mother who is always there for us, who supports us, intercedes for us and loves us so dearly.

She is our Mother, our model. She is the Mother of our Saviour. She is the Mother of the Church, She is the patroness of our nation, the Queen of Angels and Archangels, including St. Michael. She is the Mother of our families, the help of all Christians and the refuge of all of us sinners.

According to the proto-evangelium of St. James, Mary was born to the family of Saints Joachim and Anne after many years of barrenness, ceaseless prayers and good works. The arrival of Mary brought them joy, not

121

only them but the whole of humanity, because with her birth our salvation drew closer.

There are lessons we can learn from the life of our Mother Mary. We celebrate her today because she co-operated and surrendered herself to be used by God. She surrendered her entire will. Dear friends, the best way we can live is to live for God. The best thing we can do for ourselves is to surrender ourselves in service to God in any capacity possible.

Many people spend their lives in serving their wives, husbands, parents or children (family). Many serve their bosses; many spend their lives in service of a career, a profession, in an occupation, a team, a political cause. Many spend their lives in a business; a trade, in the service of a town or community but without being able to serve God.

To serve God is our primary assignment as Christians. However, our other assignments can only assume importance if they are means by which we serve God more, and not a distraction from serving God.

Mary chose to serve God with her whole life and now she is joyful for all eternity.

Celebrating her birthday

Often, I see people bringing cakes, flowers and cards to celebrate Mary's birthday. Well, it's not a bad idea. However, I suggest that we celebrate her today by paying sober attention to her messages and by obeying her different admonitions at her apparitions.

There are three things that our Mother Mary always asks of us. Let us reflect on them and obey them. I am sure they will be more pleasing to her than cakes, balloons, greeting cards and flowers.

Let us give Mary what she requests:

I.   Daily Rosary with proper meditation on the mysteries. This is the flower she wants; pray the rosary, especially for peace in the world and conversion of sinners.

II. She wants us to avoid what grieves the heart of her Son. Among other sins, she always mentions abortion, irreverence for the Holy Communion, materialism, unchastity among priests and religious, blasphemy against her Immaculate Heart, indifference to her maternal aid, immodest dressing, divorce, infidelity in marriage, widespread sexual immorality among others. Repentance from evil that offends God is the greeting card that Mary desires.

III. Mary always urges us to do penance; to make reparation and atonement for the sins with which we have grieved the heart of her Son. Penance for our sins is the birthday cake Mary desires.

As we celebrate her birthday today, let us ponder on her life and act on her words.

This is a gift far more pleasing to her than cakes, cards, flowers or even repainting her grotto.

14 SEPTEMBER

The Exaltation of the Cross
Feast

READING TEXTS:
Numbers 21:4-9; Psalm 78; Philippians 2:6-11; John 3:13-17

Today dear friends, the Holy Mother Church celebrates the feast of the Exaltation of the Cross.

This feast marks three historical events:

I.   The finding of the true Cross of Jesus by St. Helena, the mother of Emperor Constantine in 326AD.

II. Upon the re-discovery, Constantine ordered the destruction of pagan shrines and the construction of Churches at the site of the Holy Sepulchre and Mount Calvary. These Churches were dedicated on September 13th and 14th 335. It was at this point that the feast began to be celebrated in Jerusalem, on September 14th.

III. The Holy Cross was captured by the Persians in the 7th Century when they invaded Jerusalem. Later, Emperor Heraclius II defeated the Persians and the son of the Persian king assassinated his father and returned the Cross to Heraclius. Heraclius carried the Cross back to Jerusalem, to the Church on Mount Calvary. To mark this historic event, this feast became a universal celebration.

What do we celebrate today? We celebrate the power of God which turned the Cross, an emblem of shame, suffering and sorrow into an instrument of grace and salvation (Galatians 3:13). An instrument of torture

124

and curse became the instrument that reversed the curse of original sin and is now an object of veneration and a symbol of Christianity.

We celebrate the power of God to turn our shame, sorrows and pains into joy, victory and glory. The Holy Church wants us to focus on the Cross of Christ, so that our crosses in life can have meaning (Hebrews 12:2).

Just as Christ carried His old rugged Cross unto glory, we all have crosses to carry in life. For some it comes in the form of problems and crises within the family; for many people it is health challenges. Many have to bear betrayal, injustice, malice and disappointment. To some it manifests itself in challenges within their vocation. Others experience it in forms of economic hardship and for some people, it is deprivation, discrimination and persecutions on account of their faith in Jesus.

The message today is that when we carry our cross of life patiently and faithfully in union with Christ Jesus, trusting in the Father's unfailing love for us and His wise providence, we shall one day exchange it for a crown.

Our pains will one day become our gains, our sorrows will become our ticket for glory.

St. Matthew, Apostle & Evangelist

Feast

READING TEXTS:
Ephesians 4:1-7, 11-13; Psalm 19; Matthew 9:9-13

Today, the Holy Mother Church celebrates the memorial of St. Matthew; a tax collector turned a disciple and an evangelist. He wrote a Gospel account of Jesus named the 'Gospel according to St. Matthew'. Matthew eventually took the Gospel to the East precisely to Hierapolis where he was eventually martyred.

Looking at the First Reading of today, there is so much to reflect on. However, I will just focus on the latter exhortation of St. Paul. He said, *each one of us...has been given his own share of grace....*

Matthew discovered his share when he became a disciple of Jesus. We may want to ask ourselves, Have I discovered my share of grace allotted to me by Jesus Christ?.

Secondly, St. Paul explained that the gifts are to be exercised in the spirit of unity for the building of the body of Christ.

This leads us to a further meditation. Do we use our gifts to foster unity in the Church? In what ways do we put to use, our particular graces and blessings, for the building of the mystical body of Christ?

It is so important for us to allow the Holy Spirit to lead us to the truth, especially in the Church today. All the envy, tension, rivalry, schism, competitive spirit, spiritual pride and arrogance witnessed within the family of God, the Church, is a testimony that we often fail to use our gifts in the spirit of unity and with the principal motivation of building the Body of Christ.

It may not really help if we choose to continue to point fingers at others. It may be better if we all accept responsibility and seek ways to be sober and amend our ways.

Ss. Michael, Gabriel & Raphael, Archangels
Feast
———◦◦◦◦◦◦———

READING TEXTS:
Daniel 7:9-10, 13-14, Psalm 138; John 1:47-51

Today, dear friends, the Holy Mother Church celebrates the feast of the Archangels. The Archangels are the angels mentioned by name in the Bible. These are servants/messengers of God who have special roles, specially assigned to them by God in the overall plan of humanity's salvation.

The Archangels mentioned in the Bible are Michael, Gabriel and Raphael. Although some other names are collated from the apocryphal book of Enoch and in the fourth book of Esther, names like Uriel, Raguel, Sariel, Jeremiel, the Church only approves the names found in the Bible.

Michael:
Michael is the prince of the Heavenly Host (princeps militiae caelestis). He is the defender of all Christians and the Church, against the wickedness and snares of the devil. We invoke him to help us in our fight against Satan and to defend us from the assault of the devil especially at the hour of our death. St. Michael was mentioned 4 times in the Bible. Twice in Daniel, as the great prince who defends Israel against its enemies (Daniel 10:21, 12:1), once in the letter of St. Jude, with reference to his contention with the devil about the body of Moses, and finally in Revelation 12:7-12 in his

victory over Satan. His name reflects his mission Micha-el (who is like God?).

Gabriel:

Gabriel surfaced 3 times in the Scripture. First, he was explaining a vision to Daniel concerning the Messiah (Daniel 8:16 and 9:21). He then appeared to Zechariah and foretold the birth of John (Luke 1:8-20, especially verse 19). It seems very probable that he was the Angel that brought the good tidings of great joy to the shepherds keeping night watch over their flock by night (Luke 2:8-14). Angel Gabriel was also the bearer of the Good News of the incarnation of the Word of God to Mary (Luke 1:26-38). His work is to announce the message of God to whom he is sent. His name means 'strength of God' (Gaba-el).

Raphael:

Raphael was mentioned only in the book of Tobit as a wonderful healer and fellow traveller, with the young Tobias. Raphael guided Tobit's Son Tobias through a series of fantastic adventures which led to threefold happy endings, which were Tobias' marriage to Sarah, the healing of Tobit's blindness and the restoration of family fortune. According to tradition, he was the angel that stirred the waters at the healing sheep pool in Bethesda (John 5:7). He is invoked to intercede for us on our journeys and when we are ill-disposed. His name means 'Healing/Medicine of God' (Rapha-el).

Things to learn from the Archangels

Like the Archangels, we are also servants/messengers of God Let us not relent in waging war against the kingdom of Satan and all they stand for (Michael). Let us speak good words; words of hope and joy to people. Let us be a medium of good news to others

(Gabriel). Let us not neglect to care physically/ spiritually for the sick (Raphael).

In brief, let us be angels to others; ministering to their needs as the angels have ministered to ours too.

Things to do

I. Learn and pray the prayer to St. Michael the Archangel and pray it at least twice a day; morning and night.

II. Be resolved to always pray the Angelus at set-times, to recall Angel Gabriel's greetings to Mary at the annunciation. This is gradually eroding among Catholics and many say it with irreverence. They don't assume the proper prayer posture, neither do they pray it with the required meditation.

III. Visit the sick and remember to pray with them and for them for God's healing.

IV. Read the book of Tobit (14 chapters).

Call your parents today, your guardian, an elderly person. Wish them God's blessings. Let them know that God loves and cares for them.

St. Luke, Evangelist

Feast

READING TEXTS:
2 Timothy 4:10-17; Psalm 145; Luke 10:1-9

Today, the Holy Mother Church celebrates the feast of St. Luke. St. Luke is one of the four Gospel Evangelists. In fact, he was the only Gentile Evangelist. The early Church Fathers ascribed to him the authorship of both the Gospel according to Luke and the Acts of the Apostles.

Luke was a physician (Colossians 4:14) and a well-educated man. He was converted to Christianity and he became Paul's companion/disciple in his second missionary journey (Philemon 1:24, 2 Timothy 4:11 the First Reading). In fact, he was with Paul until he (Paul) suffered martyrdom. Luke was reportedly hanged on an olive tree in Boeotia, Greece at the age of 84 years. Five things stand out clearly in Luke's Gospel account:

I.   It is a Gospel of God's mercy and the compassion of Jesus, as reflected in his numerous healing narratives and the parables of Jesus concerning God's Mercy.

II. It is called the Gospel of the Holy Spirit. It pays detailed attention to the presence and actions of the Holy Spirit in the life and ministry of Jesus and others.

III. It is called a Gospel of women. This is because Luke gave due attention to women. Luke recognised women as disciples of Jesus and gave pride of place to Mary as the mother of Jesus and the Church.

IV. It is a Gospel of prayer. Luke showed a marked interest in the private prayer life of Jesus and in His parables on prayer.

V. It is a Gospel of praise, paying attention to the many songs offered in praise of God; the Benedictus, Ave Maria, Magnificat, Gloria and the Nunc Dimittis of Simeon.

Message for us today

Let us take one lesson from Luke as a person and one from his Gospel:

I. Jesus called all classes of people, the learned and the unlettered, Jews and non-Jews. He wants all of us to use our gifts, charism, knowledge and skills for the service of the Good News. Jesus needs us as much as He needed Luke. The harvest remains plentiful and there is always need for more labourers in the vineyard. Let us continue to ask God to open our eyes to see further ways in which we can be productive in His vineyard, further ways we can contribute to the growth of God's kingdom. We should never complain of doing too much already because we can never do enough for God.

II. Let us learn, from the Lucan presentation of Jesus, the need to be compassionate and merciful to others. We should not be part of the injustice, evil, wickedness, insensitivity that characterises societal consciousness today. We are invited to have a heart like Christ; like Luke, who paid attention to those at the margins of the society, the sick, the poor, women and children, care for these people should not escape our attention. According to St. Lawrence, *they   are the greatest treasures of the Church.*

Through the intercessions of St Luke, may our lives become another wonderful account of the Gospel of Jesus.

St. Simon and St. Jude, Apostles

Feast

READING TEXTS:
Ephesians 2:19-22; Psalm 19; Luke 6:12-16

Today, we celebrate the feast of two of Jesus' Apostles; Saints Simon the Zealot and Jude Thaddeus, son of James.

They were not as well-known as Peter, James and John but nonetheless, as we have heard in today's Gospel, they were also called by Jesus to participate in His ministry.

Simon is described as 'the Zealot'. He was from Cana. The Zealots were extreme Jewish nationalists who were always against the authority of the Romans. They believed that the Jews were meant to be free, independent and a uniquely 'theocratic' nation. As such, they were like terrorists, who raided and killed both Romans, and Jews who were collaborating with the Romans (especially tax collectors) and they were always causing insurrection targeted against the Romans.

St. Jude is also called Thaddeus. He is often referred to as the patron of desperate cases or the 'saint of last resort' because of his name. He bore the same name as the notorious Judas Iscariot. He is regarded as the author of the epistle of St. Jude, which was written to warn brethren about the destructiveness of heresy.

According to tradition, they went to preach in Mesopotamia and Persia; they converted the Persian king, King Tridate III and about 60,000 Persians and built churches over the ancient ruins of the idolatrous temples. They were eventually martyred by pagans in that territory. Simon was cut in two with a saw and Jude's throat was cut with a spear in about 65AD.

Two lessons from the lives of Simon and Jude

I.   Looking at the Gospel of today, we see unlikely people in the list of Jesus' disciples. For instance, we see a crooked tax collector (Matthew), an impetuous fisherman (Peter), two short-tempered fellows called 'sons of thunder' (James and John), a lover of money (Judas), the tribalistic Nathaniel, and a militant/political thug (Simon). God saw all their imperfections and yet found them 'use-able'.

Anyone can be useful to God, despite their weaknesses and imperfections. I don't know the name of the musician who sang this song, but I remember the message of the song. He said that if God can use the jawbone of a donkey to win victory for Samson, against the Philistines (Judges 15:15-16), then He can use anything/anyone including you.

Our weaknesses do not disqualify us, just as we are not qualified by our merits. If only we are willing, then the transforming grace of God will turn our weaknesses to strength.

II. Simon and Jude were not as well-known as some of the other 'popular' disciples, but they were also working for the establishment of God's kingdom.

The First Reading tells us that we are no longer aliens, but members of God's household. It means that we are also called to the service of the kingdom.

Like Simon and Jude, we may not be very popular, or do what is visible to all, but then in our own little way, we must keep doing something for God. We are called to faithful service and not popularity.

You may not be a deacon or an extra-ordinary minister of Holy Communion, you may not be a teacher of RCIA, you may not be in the parish pastoral council, you might not have stood before the lectern before, but then there are other less visible and effective ways we can serve God.

For instance, you may just be a noise-less peacemaker, a person who notices people who are absent in Church and checks on them. You may be someone who makes people feel loved; appreciating people's efforts, encouraging people who are struggling and alerting the priests to parishioners who may need pastoral help. You may clean the dirty pews and spaces in the Church or help children to be calm at Mass. You may be someone who spreads the message of the Divine Mercy to people, shares the beauty of the Rosary, makes reparations for sins committed against Jesus in the Holy Eucharist. Maybe you are committed to always bringing an elderly man or woman to Church each Sunday or interpreting the message for someone who is struggling with the language.

These are simple, noise-less but very effective ways of working for Christ and building His kingdom here on earth.

The God who sees everything that is done in secret will reward all our labours of love (Hebrews 6:10).

The Solemnity of All Saints

Solemnity

READING TEXTS: *Revelation 7:2-4, 9-14; Psalm 24; 1 John 3:1-3; Matthew 5:1-12*

The month of October is specially dedicated to the Blessed Virgin Mary. The month of October was also observed as an extra-ordinary month of mission.

Today is the first day of the month of November. The month of November is specially set aside to remember and pray for members of the Church-suffering and to also ask for prayers from members of the triumphant-church. In other words, it is a month set apart to remember all the faithful departed.

We start this in a very beautiful way by remembering all those who are in heaven. Who are they? How did they get there?

Who are they?

There is a temptation to see the Saints as 3rd century monks or 11th century Franciscan nuns; as people who lived in caves and spent their whole lives in cloisters. Yet the First Reading says they are a huge number of people from every nation, race, tribe and language and they are now dressed in white, holding palm branches, worshipping God day and night.

They are our relatives, friends, grandparents, family members, children, youths, colleagues. Some of them were also in this parish; some of them we attended their funerals. Many of them were uncanonized but they are now in heaven.

While on earth, they faced the same temptations we are facing now. They suffered as much as many of us are suffering now. Some of them died of sicknesses very common among us today. They had the same family and personal struggles we are having. Some of them also asked God, why?.

So how did they make it to heaven?

Despite all they went through, they never lost faith in God. They suffered great persecutions, their faith was tried, they were ridiculed, they lost the friendship of the world but never lost faith in God: the greatest loss in life is to lose faith in God.

They never stopped loving God. They loved God above all things; above family and friends, above the promises of this world, God came first in their lives; they loved God even more than their lives (Revelation 12:11). Like St. Paul, they declared that nothing would separate them from loving God. Despite all they went through, their hunger and thirst for God was never vanquished or suppressed, theirs was perfect love.

They never stopped hoping. Just as St. John says in the Second Reading, they entertained the hope of future glory and it kept them still. They kept the hope of eternal happiness with God before their eyes just like Jesus who, because of the joy ahead, endured the Cross. They endured the worst temptation, trials and agony of the world, knowing that the glory promised is incomparably greater (Hebrews 12:2; Romans 8:18).

Let us take note that they didn't make it to heaven simply because they died. I need to clarify this with all passion, charity and clarity. Death does not automatically make one a Saint or transport one to a place of refreshment, light and peace. Eternal happiness is largely made possible by God's grace and mercy, but it is consequent upon the choices we make in life.

What do they enjoy in heaven?

The Second Reading of today from St. John gives us a hint. They have been crowned, decorated and revealed as sons and daughters of God. They enjoy the fullest revelation of the glory of adoption into God's family. They no longer cry, suffer, complain or mourn. Their sicknesses have disappeared, their pains gone, their sorrows vanished, and they now praise God day and night.

Their knowledge is perfected, hope confirmed, faith rewarded, and love compensated.

The greatest joy they have is that they now see God face to face, just as I see you now. I can't even imagine their joy; with their glorified eyes they see the fullness of the glory of God! Hallelujah!

Their greatest wish?

That you and I will one day be with them.

As we ask for their intercession today, let us not get tired in our journey. Let us continue to make efforts as we rely on grace and mercy. Let us keep heaven in mind in all that we do, for to lose heaven is to lose everything. To gain heaven is the only reason our existence can make sense.

Commemoration of All the Faithful Departed

(All Souls' Day)

READING TEXTS: *Wisdom 3:1-9, Psalm 23, Romans 5:5-11; Mark 15:33-39, 16:1-6*

Yesterday we joyfully celebrated the solemnity of All Saints. We praised God for our brethren who are now enjoying the blessedness of heaven. Today's liturgy is more sober in nature. We turn to God asking for mercy for our brethren who have also departed this world but who are yet to attain the perfection required to enter into the joy of heaven. These are souls undergoing purification in purgatory.

It is true that many people do not believe in purgatory and many do not understand what it is. The most vivid biblical reference we have is the book of 2 Maccabees 12:38-45 (which is not in the Bible of other non-Catholic Christians). However, in 1 Corinthians 15:29, St. Paul made reference to the practice of being baptised on behalf of the dead, which presupposes some form of intercession for the dead.

In any case, many holy men and women and even ordinary people have received countless apparitions and visions about purgatory, and some were even directly asked for prayers by souls in purgatory. These apparitions are so real and numerous that it will be impossible to dismiss them simply as phantoms.

Let me just quote something from the diary of St. Maria Faustina:

140

> *I saw my Guardian Angel, who ordered me to*
> *follow him. In a moment I was in a misty place*
> *full of fire in which there was a great crowd of*
> *suffering souls. They were praying fervently,*
> *but to no avail, for themselves; only we can*
> *come to their aid. The flames which were*
> *burning them did not touch me at all. My*
> *Guardian Angel did not leave me for an instant.*
> *I asked these souls what their greatest suffering*
> *was. They answered me in one voice that their*
> *greatest torment was longing for God. I saw*
> *Our Lady visiting the souls in Purgatory. The*
> *souls call her "The Star of the Sea." She brings*
> *them refreshment. I wanted to talk with them*
> *some more, but my Guardian Angel beckoned*
> *me to leave. We went out of that prison of*
> *suffering. [I heard an interior voice] which*
> *said, My mercy does not want this, but justice*
> *demands it.   Since that time, I am in closer*
> *communion with the suffering souls. (Diary, 20)*

Who are those in purgatory?

They are human beings like us. They are people we know: friends, members of our families, colleagues, our grandparents, clergymen and nuns, people who were in the same pious societies with us, our neighbours, some of them were our Facebook friends, people who once liked   our pictures and commented on our posts. They were like us, but they have been called from this world.

Why are they in purgatory?

I.   They died in the state of venial sin.
II.   They are souls who have not finished atoning for the temporal punishments due to mortal sins, whose guilt has been removed after a good confession, but the punishment has not been fully satisfied'.

III. They are people who had genuine love for God, but their love was imperfect. They lived good lives; they were saints-in-the-making but never fully attained the sanctity that qualifies for the beatific vision.

Will everyone go there?

No! God in His grace and mercy will perfect the love of many and will enable them to fully satisfy their temporal punishments; mostly through sufferings, sicknesses and tribulation. Some souls will escape the pains of purgatory and be transported straight to heaven.

Duration in purgatory

This depends on the nature and number of venial sins and the punishment un-atoned for. According to Fr. F.X Schouppe, S.J. in his book 'Purgatory Explained', some spend as much as two hundred years there. However, one minute in purgatory is like a year of intense pains and suffering on earth.

How can we relieve their sufferings?

By prayers and good works offered for them; through the Mass, which is the highest of all prayers; praying before the Blessed Sacrament, the Crucifix or statue of our Mother Mary for the souls in purgatory; by giving alms for their sake, praying the rosary, Stations of the Cross, for example.

Now what are we to do?

Let us do all we can while we can, to remember souls in purgatory and to pray and work for their relief and release. If possible, we could pray for them daily. This is the greatest act of kindness.

We may offer up our sicknesses, pains and disappointments to God in union with Christ in atonement for our sins and the relief of souls in purgatory. This is the redemptive value of suffering.

Let us always atone for our sins and do regular penance. This is always the message of our Lady in her apparitions, but unfortunately many are not aware of this because it is not preached. Often, it is scarcely preached.

And most importantly:

Let us be careful enough to wage war not only against mortal sins, but also venial faults. Some of the sins we take for granted like making noise in the church, lack of reverence for the Blessed Sacrament, loose talk, neglect of prayers, coming late to church out of indifference and carelessness, delay in forgiveness, indecent dressing, willful distraction in prayers, and other sins are what people spend years atoning for in purgatory.

May the souls of all the Faithful departed, through the mercy of God, rest in peace.

Amen.

The Dedication of Lateran Basilica

Feast

READING TEXTS: *Ezekiel 47:1-2,8-9,12; Psalm 46; 1 Corinthians 3:9-11, 16-17; John 2:13-22*

Today the Universal Church celebrates the feast of the Dedication of the Lateran Basilica.

This feast, as simple as it seems, is very profound and relevant for us as Christians/Catholics. Historically, we celebrate the first public place of worship built by Emperor Constantine (the first Christian Emperor) for Christians to worship. This place of worship was built on land given to him by the wealthy Lateran family. This is why it is called the Lateran Basilica.

The Lateran Basilica is the seat of the Pope, the Cathedral of Rome, the oldest basilica. It is called the mother of all Christian churches. It is also, as it were, the parish of all Catholics (Omnium urbis et orbis ecclesiarum mater, et caput   the mother of all the churches in the city and in the world and their head).

It was dedicated to the Most Holy Saviour on the 9th November 324 by Pope St. Sylvester. In the 10th Century, Pope Sergius III dedicated it to St. John the Baptist and Pope Lucius II dedicated it to St. John the Evangelist in the 12th Century. This feast has been celebrated in Rome since the dedication and, in the 12th Century, it was extended to the whole Roman rite as a sign of unity and love towards the See of Peter.

144

Significance and meaning of today's feast

I.   This feast celebrates our communion with the Church of Rome; our particular Church is not disconnected from the Mother Church. We are part of the Church that was built by Christ on Peter and with the Pope as the successor of Peter. In this feast, we celebrate the unity of the One, Holy, Roman Catholic and apostolic Church.

When we draw this to our immediate context, there is no particular church or parish that is hypostatical (self-subsisting). We are part of a universal Church. As such, no Church can generate her own liturgy, culture or her own brand of Catholicism. No parish should feel they are not responsible or related to the One Church. Every Church must exist in communion and not in isolation.

II.   From the First Reading, we are reminded that the Church is a Holy Place; a place where God dwells (Habakkuk2:20). It is The house of God (Domus Dei). From there, grace, blessing and power flows. As such, we must therefore not lose this sense of mystery whenever we enter the Church.

When we understand this, it reflects in the way we dispose ourselves, in what we do in the Church and even in how we appear in God's house.

One of the sacrilegious acts I have observed in this country is that Churches with the Blessed Sacrament are being used for dancing, drinking, parties, and funfairs. It reminds me of what Daniel talked about (in Daniel 11:31,12:11): the abomination that causes desolation (*ha-shikkutsmeshomem*).

III. In the Second Reading, St. Paul introduces a personal dimension to today's feast. He tells us that we are God's temple and God's Spirit dwells in us. This means that our hearts should be a place where we worship God, meditate on God and encounter God. Like Jesus purified the temple in today's Gospel, let us also cleanse our heart of every transaction that renders it un-befitting for God to dwell. Let us make a whip by fasting, prayer, penance, self-denial and the dismantling of every tent of pride, hatred, enmity, jealousy, anger, lust, avarice, all evil thoughts and desires.

Let us pray

Lord Jesus, I renew my self-dedication to you today. Take me as I am; purify me and make me a worthy and holy temple fit for you.

Amen.

The Lord Jesus Christ, the King of the Universe

Solemnity

READING TEXTS: *2 Samuel 5:1-3; Psalm 122; Colossians 1:12-20; Luke 23:35-43*

Today is the last Sunday in Ordinary time, year C; the Holy Mother Church celebrates the feast of Christ the Universal King.

By way of history, this feast was instituted by Pope Pius XI in an encyclical titled *Quas Primas*. This encyclical was written shortly after World War I to address some of the challenges that arose from that war. One was the fact that many people were beginning to lose faith in God and question His existence or Lordship in the face of so much loss, suffering, hunger, hardship, destruction, violence and death. It was an age that witnessed the rise of secularism, anti-clericalism and nationalism.

Secondly, many authoritarian leaders emerged, and they claimed to have absolute power and authority, presenting themselves as the solution to the people's problems. They were arrogant and hostile to faith, God and religion. These leaders included Adolf Hitler (leader of the Nazi party), Benito Mussolini, who was a fascist dictator and Joseph Stalin of the Soviet Union.

Pope Pius XI wanted to remind the world through this feast that:

I.   All power and authority belong to Christ. He is the King of Kings and the whole of humankind is

147

subject to His Power (n18). Every other leader is bound to honour and obey Him. He is the one who will come again as King to judge every other leader, ruler, king or subject.

II.   To remind the world that there can be no lasting peace except by submitting to the reign of Christ. The opening paragraph of the encyclical reads:

The   evils in the world were due to the fact that the majority of men had thrust Jesus Christ and His holy law out of their lives... as long as individuals and states refused to submit to the rule of our Saviour, there would be no really hopeful prospect of a lasting peace among nations.

III. The last Sunday was chosen because, according to the encyclical in n29, the feast of the Kingship of Christ sets the crowning glory upon the mysteries of the life of Christ already commemorated during the liturgical year.

Three points for us to ponder on today:

I.   *True peace is in accepting the reign of Christ.*
     Peace is something very scarce in society today, in families and in people's lives. The evil in our societies today is a reflection of the lack of peace in people's hearts. How many families today are actually living in true peace?

     The feast of today reminds us that, if we surrender our lives to the Lordship of Christ, if we intentionally enthrone Jesus in our families and honour and obey Him, we shall experience true peace and joy (read John 14:27). His reign is the reign of peace.

     Every family on earth has an *invisible throne* and it is always being occupied. What goes on in the family points to who occupies the throne.

Many families are in mess today because the devil is the one on the throne. In paragraph 20, Pope Pius stated: *oh, what happiness would be ours if all individuals and families would but let themselves be governed by Christ... then at length will many evils be cured; peace with all its blessings be restored.*

II.   The use of power.

As we celebrate the feast of Christ as King, we are being led to reflect on power and how it ought to be exercised. Christ is the King of the whole world. His reign is timeless and everlasting, His kingdom has no boundary or jurisdiction, His authority has no limit; it reaches beyond heaven and on earth just as today's Second Reading testifies. Despite this, He rules with love and humility. He welcomes the weak. In today's Gospel He bore insults patiently and forgave sinners; He is a servant King. This is the type of king that He is.

This is a lesson for all of us who exercise any form of authority or occupy a position of leadership. Let us learn from the example of our King and exercise our authority with kindness, goodness, patience, humility and most especially mercy.

III.   Our identity.

Because Christ is our King, spiritually we are all members of a royal family. The Second Reading puts it more succinctly *"He has taken us out of the power of darkness and created a place for us in the kingdom of the Son that He loves.*

We are princes and princesses of the Kingdom of Christ. This implies at least two things:

i. We ought to live as royal/kingly people. We must talk, behave and think like citizens of God's kingdom. We must obey the laws of His kingdom of grace and holiness, truth and life (1 Peter 2:9).

ii. We must keep in mind that our kingdom is not of this world (John 18:36) and so we must look less for consolation in this world and set our hearts on the Kingdom of Heaven, where there is lasting peace, joy, freedom and eternal glory. This is why Jesus taught us to say: 'adveniat regnum tuum' (your kingdom come).

St. Andrew, Apostle

Feast

———— ❦❦❦ ————

WE NEED MORE ANDREWS

READING TEXTS:
Romans 10:9-18; Psalm 19; Matthew 4:18-22

After a Sunday Mass, I was asking a familiar parishioner why she came in late. She told me: I was welcoming people. I found that interesting, as prior to that, I had never taken note of the ministry of the 'welcomers'. The 'welcomers' stand at the entrance door of the Church, to welcome people to the Church; sometimes they show newcomers where to sit and hand them a hymn book or newsletter. I think this is a wonderful ministry, if we understand the Mass as a banquet of the Lord. We need those who will welcome people to the feast.

However, more than those who will welcome people to the Church, we urgently need those who will introduce and welcome others to Jesus. We need today, more than ever before, people who by their choice of words, the fragrance of their character, authenticity of piety, the depth of their zeal, the kindness of their hearts and fervent evangelical spirit will lead others to Jesus. Many people are far from the Lord; many are walking away from the Lord and many do not even know Him. Unfortunately, sometimes we Christians act like the disciples who were stopping people from seeing Jesus (Mark 10:13-16).

This message is timely, as today we celebrate the feast of St. Andrew.

151

St. Andrew

According to today's Gospel, Andrew was one of the first to be called by Jesus to be His disciple. Andrew was a fisherman from Bethsaida. His name means 'manly' or 'courageous' and true to his name, he courageously followed Jesus. According to an ancient tradition, Andrew preached the Gospel in various places, until eventually he suffered death on an X-shaped Cross in Greece.

What is Andrew known for? Andrew didn't write a book within the Bible and no page of the Bible recorded his preaching, but he was known for introducing people to Jesus. He became what he was called to be ἡλιεῖςἡνθρώπων (halieisanthrōpōn), a fisher of men.

According to the account of St. John, he first introduced his brother Peter to Jesus (John 1:41-42). Later, he introduced the boy with five barley loaves and two fish to Jesus (John 6:8-9). Again, together with Philip, he introduced the Greeks to Jesus (John 12:20-22). Eventually, he went to Greece to introduce Jesus to the Greeks in their territory.

Interestingly, he is the last Saint we celebrate at the end of the liturgical year and this is significant. Andrew continues to introduce us to Jesus, whose coming we anticipate through the advent preparation.

Our world needs more bearers of the Good News to others. We need more fishers of men and women; we need more Christians who are passionate about bringing wandering souls to Jesus. We need more ANDREWS.

Immaculate Conception of the Blessed Virgin Mary

Solemnity

————

READING TEXTS: *Genesis 3:9-15,20; Psalm 98; Ephesians 1:3-6,11-12; Luke 1:26-38*

The main theme of Advent is 'prepare', and I think everybody understands this albeit differently.

Everyone is actually preparing but for different things. Many are only preparing for the Christmas travel, party, shopping and visit. However, we are meant to use this time to prepare for Christ, so that at Christmas He will be reborn in our hearts as He was born in the manger two thousand years ago.

Today is the feast of the Immaculate Conception. This feast simply tells us how God prepared for Christmas. He prepared for the coming of His Son by preserving a woman free from the stains of original sin. So, while we decorate our homes, God decorated the womb of a woman, so that the One who was to save us from sin would be conceived in a womb preserved from sin. The one who was to restore our human nature to its original innocence, shared in a human nature that was perfect, innocent and unstained by sin.

This doctrine, which was almost universally believed over the centuries, was proclaimed a dogma in 1854 by Pope Pius IX. To confirm this doctrine, four years after the proclamation, precisely on March 25, 1858, Our Lady appeared to St. Bernadette at Lourdes

153

and pronounced her name as the Immaculate Conception.

It may interest us to know that even the Quran shares the doctrine of how God chose, prepared and purified Mary:

And [mention] when the angels said, O Mary, indeed Allah has chosen you and purified you and chosen you above the women of the worlds. Surah Ali-Imran 3:42

In today's Gospel, the Angel told Mary, *Rejoice, so highly favoured! The Lord is with you.* 'Highly favoured' here means full of grace, and the highest grace is to be preserved from sin. When Mary also sang her Magnificat in Luke 1:49, she said *the Almighty has done great things for me...* The greatest thing that was done for her was to preserve her from sin.

So as today, we rejoice in the wisdom, love and goodness of God made manifest in Mary, let us also keep these two things in mind:

I. Let us learn from this solemnity, how we ought to prepare for Christ's coming. God prepared Mary, not by making her the most beautiful, intelligent, wise or eloquent woman, but by preserving her from sin.

    This tells us that to prepare for the coming of Christ at Christmas too, our primary focus should be to purify our own hearts from sin. It goes back to the message of repentance of John the Baptist in the wilderness. We prepare by honest examination of conscience, true sorrow for sins and firm purpose of amendment, good confession, penance and living good lives under the power of grace.

II. The Second Reading of today tells us that like Mary, we have also been blessed with rich spiritual blessings in Christ, chosen before the world was made. Chosen to be what?

- To be holy and spotless.
- To become adopted sons and daughters
- Chosen for His praise and greater glory.

What a beautiful plan the Lord has for each of us! But are we living and flourishing in that pre-determined plan?

Let us have recourse to our Blessed Mother and ask for her intercession, so that we may not relent in our battle against sin and we may live for the praise and glory of Him who has chosen and adopted us for His Glory.

Christmas Day

Solemnity

I WISH IT COULD BE CHRISTMAS EVERYDAY

READING TEXTS:
At dawn: *Isaiah 62:11-12; Psalm 97:1, 6, 11-12; 2 Titus*
                  ***Acclamation:** Luke 2:14; **Gospel:** Luke 2:15-20*
Mass (daytime): *Isaiah 52:7-10; Psalm 98:1, 2-3ab, 3cd-4, 5-6; Hebrews 1:1-6 **Gospel:** John 1:1-18.*

I have been asking people what they love most about Christmas and I have received many different answers. Some said they love to see Santa Claus, some children told me they love the fireworks and the travels to see their family. Of course, as expected, many love the Christmas turkey and roasts, the carols and nativity plays, plenty of chocolates, the Christmas party and the presents from friends and parents.

A woman once told me, I don't like Christmas. Actually, there is no one who knows the true meaning of Christmas, who won't love Christmas. What I think she was referring to is the stress we cause ourselves, and the financial crises we plunge ourselves into, which in actual fact are not the real essence of Christmas.

Can you pause briefly and ask yourself what you really love about Christmas? You don't need to give 'spiritual' responses on this matter, just be real.

Well, let me tell you five things I love most about Christmas and don't laugh or judge me.

156

I.   The Christmas songs, I mean the carols, I really love
     Christmas carols and my favourite is 'Adeste
     Fidelis.
     Adeste, fideles,
     Laeti triumphantes,
     Venite, venite in Bethlehem!
     Natum videte,
     Regem angelorum
     Venite, adoremus!
     Venite, adoremus!
     Venite, adoramus Dominum!
     Venite, adoramus Dominum!

II. I love the beautiful Christmas decorations; sometimes
     I drive around the town to see some of the beautiful
     Christmas lights and decorations.

III. I love the exchange of gifts. I have received so many
     boxes of chocolates, shortbread, and cards (and
     some of these cards contain coloured paper with the
     head of the Queen on!).

IV. I love the fact that Christmas brings families together.
     In this country, everyone is extremely busy working
     long hours, but at Christmas, many of us are able to
     take a break and meet up with those members of our
     families that we haven't seen for a while.

V.   I love the fact that at Christmas, people who haven't
     been to Church return to the Church. I think this is
     what I love most. I was asking my barber if he is a
     Christian. He said: yes,   and with an aura of pride,
     he added: I   go to church at Christmas and Easter.

     This morning I was listening to a song by Wizzard
entitled: I   wish it could be Christmas every day   and

this inspired the title of my homily today. I do wish it could be Christmas every day. I wish the Christmas spirit could last longer. Many people, however, might object to this idea.

We might object because Christmas, for us, is associated with lots of expenses and stress. Actually, Christmas is not meant to be expensive and it is something we can celebrate every day. We can keep the Christmas spirit alive even after the Christmas festival.

How?

i.   We can sing beautiful songs of praise to God daily. Our carols don't have to be sung only at Christmas. The Psalmist says: *I will bless the Lord at all times, His praise always on my lips* (Psalm 34:1).When we do this, we prolong the spirit of Christmas.

ii.   We can give gifts to people not just for Christmas but every day. The greatest gifts are not even material or tangible. Gifts are not just chocolates and stuff from Marks and Spencer. We can give more patience to someone who provokes us, forgiveness to someone who doesn't deserve it and kind words to someone discouraged. We can also appreciate someone whose struggles are going unnoticed, smile to encourage someone who is downcast and spend time listening to someone's life-stories. When we do this, we prolong the spirit of Christmas.

We can even make ourselves a gift to others; a gift to our family, a gift to our friends and the people we work with (there are people in this parish who I see as God's gift to encourage me). When we do this, we prolong the spirit of Christmas.

iii.   We may choose not to wait until Christmas to show our love of and care for our families. The most beautiful Christmas tree is a family gathered together with joy and love. What if we show how much we cherish our families, in concrete ways, even outside of Christmas? When we do this, we prolong the spirit of Christmas.

iv.   We may decide to decorate our homes, not just for Christmas, but throughout the year. Peace makes a home brighter than any Christmas lights. Love is more beautiful than a Christmas tree; a home characterised by kindness and good communication is the best carol. Love, peace, unity and good communications are precious, beautiful decorations. When we do this, we prolong the spirit of Christmas.

We may also set time aside for God, not only on Christmas Day but on other days too. God wishes to see you more frequently than once or twice a year. In the spirit of Christmas, you may set aside more time for God. Whenever we come to Church, we celebrate something of Christmas, because Christmas is the reason, we are Christians.

St. Stephen, Martyr

Feast

READING TEXTS:
Acts 6:8-10, 7:54-59; Psalm 31; Matthew 10:17-22

Today, the Holy Mother Church celebrates the martyrdom of St. Stephen. St. Stephen is called the proto martyr, that is, the first to suffer martyrdom among the believers of the early Church.

Who was St. Stephen?

We find Stephen's story in Acts 6 and 7. St. Stephen was a deacon in the early Church. He is described in today's First Reading as a man filled with grace and power, who worked miracles and signs among the people. Out of jealousy, some learned Jews came from Cyrene and Alexandria, Cilicia and Asia (these were centres of great intellectual activity), to debate with him. It was a contest of human knowledge and the knowledge that the Holy Spirit bestows, a match between human learning and revelation. Stephen didn't just outshine them in knowledge, he was also blessed with a vision beyond their cognitive capacities; a vision that ridiculed the very foundation of their theology. Given this, they resorted to violence and murder to stop him.

As we reflect on the martyrdom of St. Stephen, let us pray today for those of our brothers and sisters who are being intentionally discriminated against and persecuted on account of their faith. Across the world, in

160

many countries, Christians are still being ill-treated and massacred at genocidal levels.

In Sudan, anyone who converts from Islam to Christianity is charged with apostasy and is placed on death row. Terrorist suicide bombings on three Churches in Sri Lanka (on 21st April 2019, Easter Sunday) left hundreds dead and wounded. There is also a progressive increase in the persecution of Christians, especially in the Middle East, Asia and North Africa.

We pray that God will grant fortitude to His children and come to their aid in their misery. May St. Stephen intercede for all Christians who are suffering persecution and institutional discrimination.

It is noticeable that St. Stephen was surrounded by bitter, angry and violent people and yet, he refused to be intimidated by them. Rather, he focused on heaven and he received a revelation that brought him great consolation in the midst of his tribulations.

Often, we focus on the wrong things in life. We focus on people; setting our minds on what they will think of us, what they will say or do to us and then we exhaust ourselves seeking approval, looking for the friendship of the world.

St. Stephen has taught us to focus on heaven; to be concerned about seeking God's face   His glory and approval (Psalm 121). The more we learn to focus on God, the more we are unmoved by the terror around us, the intimidation of people or the vanity of fleeting praises.

The Holy Family of Jesus, Mary and Joseph

Feast

READING TEXTS: *Sirach 3:3-7, 14-17; Psalm 128; Colossians 3:12-21; Matthew 2:13-15, 19-23*

Today is the feast of the Holy Family: the family of Jesus, Mary and Joseph. It is also a day the Church has specially set aside for three things:

- To thank God for the gift of our families.
- To pray for peace and healing in families having difficulties and troubles.
- To reflect on the state of our families.

Today, I want us to pray especially for those who are orphaned or widowed, for those who are separated or divorced; that they may know the love and kindness of the Lord and that our Blessed Mother will support them in their difficulties.

My heart goes out to those whose spouses are neither practicing the faith nor encouraging them in their faith. This again is another challenge; I commend to you the prayers of St. Monica, who bore a similar Cross. May her prayers help you to find inner strength and grace.

On this day, it is customary that we read our Bishop's pastoral letter and so I will just mention some short points for us to reflect on:

I. *A family is God's gift and we are all responsible to God as to how we govern it.*

162

Some people prioritise their jobs, friendships and ambition over their families. The highest calling of a man and woman is to build a good family, marriage and home.

Parents have the important responsibility of nurturing Godly children (Proverbs 22:6). Sometimes, due to no fault of our own, our children stray; let us not relent in praying for them. Our society is so complex these days and so it is increasingly difficult to build Godly children. A man or woman who thrives in his/her career and neglects the duty of building a good home with Godly children cannot be called successful.

II.   A family is meant to be a domestic church.

The mark of a Christian family is that it is a domestic Church where faith is nurtured. It is not enough to go to a family club or to go on vacation or to the cinema together. A family should have time occasionally, and intentionally, to come together to pray and share the Word of God.

No one can raise a good family these days without the help of the Lord. Every family is targeted by the devil, who will try to break, destroy and reduce it to ruin. It is through the power of consistent prayers and the bulwark of faith that we can resist the assailant.

It is time for men to honour their responsibilities as the high priest in the family. A husband is not just a protector and provider; he is also a priest and prophet, who mediates God's blessings to his children. How many fathers in this Church still lead at prayer and impart God's blessings upon their children?

III.   A family is a place of forgiveness.

There is no perfect family anywhere. In the family of Adam and Eve, Cain their first-born son killed his brother Abel. In the family of David, the ancestor of Jesus, there are tales of deception, adultery, incest, rape, betrayal, scandals etc.

In today's Gospel, we see the challenges of the Holy Family of Nazareth; they were once homeless or at least fugitives in Egypt. Stress and tensions are a huge part of the home today with the pressures of work, time and finances coupled with the stress that comes from raising children. Many people get so stressed with the bills or the direct debit payments that are coming out of their bank accounts. In the midst of all these, we must fight for our families to survive.

What about conflicts and disagreements? These are all parts of family struggles and challenges we have to deal with in building a good family. One of the ways we can fight for our family is through forgiveness. The frequencies of domestic violence and spousal homicides today are unacceptable. Most of these are borne out of hatred, unchecked anger and retaliation.

Some people still hold grudges against their spouses for wrongs committed prior to marriage or many years ago (1 Corinthians 13:6). Forgiveness is important, not just for those who are married, but also those who are separated from their spouses for whatever reasons, just or unjust. We must beg God for the grace of forgiveness.

IV. Children are meant to be blessings in the family.

I won't end this reflection without saying speaking directly to the children here today. A child is meant to be a blessing and a source of happiness to their parents (Psalm 127:3). Be a wise and a blessed child. What makes a wise child?

i. *Gratitude/appreciation of parents.*
    After Mass last Sunday, a girl told me to tell her mother that she loves her and that she sees all her sacrifices and courage and said that I should bless her mother. As I was telling the mum she couldn't stop crying. A good child appreciates their parents.

ii. *The most fundamental quality of a sensible child is obedience.*
    Unfortunately, many children today are rebellious. In some homes I have visited, I have observed that many children are only disposed to say, No,   Why?   I don't want to... Some children lack basic respect for their parents, do not exhibit civil behaviours or basic ethics and manners. What some of us call civilisation is damnation, a testimony to parental failure.

May I repeat the words of the First Reading:

Whoever   respects his father is atoning for his sins; he who honours his mother is like someone amassing a fortune.

Whoever respects his father will be happy with children of his own...he who sets his mother at ease is showing obedience to the Lord.

May God bless our families and teach us how to build the foundation on the solid rock that is Christ.

St. John the Evangelist, Apostle

Feast

READING TEXTS:
1 John 1: 1-4; Psalm 97; John 20:2-

Today, the Holy Mother Church celebrates the feast of St. John the Evangelist. John was the brother of James the Greater, and they were sons of Zebedee. John had a special place in the Apostolic College. He is described as, *the disciple whom Jesus loved* (cf. John 13, 23; 19:26; 20, 2; 21,7. 20). He is one of the three principal witnesses to some extraordinary events in the ministry of Christ; for instance, the raising of the daughter of Jairus, the Transfiguration and the agony in the garden of Gethsemane. He had the privilege of reclining next to Jesus, lying close to the breast of Jesus (John 13:25) at the last supper.

When Jesus was arrested, all the disciples deserted Him and fled (Matthew 26, 56). Only Peter and John followed Jesus and John became the only one among them at the foot of the Cross (John 19:26). It was to him that Jesus entrusted His Mother (vs. 26-27).

St. John is the author of the fourth Gospel. He also wrote three Epistles and the Book of Revelation.

According to the Gospel account of today, he was a principal witness of the resurrection. Later, we learnt that he was exiled to Patmos where he wrote the book of Revelation (cf. Revelation 1, 9). John was a confessor who followed the Lord from his youth and also grew in faith and love until his death.

Like John, let us seek to grow deeper in our relationship with the Lord. Many people are satisfied with the basics of religion: coming to church whenever it is convenient, participating in parish fayres and helping in basic things when they are called upon. This does not exhaust what it means to be a Christian.

The essence of Christianity/religion is relationship. This is what John enjoyed with the Lord; an intimate, lively and transforming relationship with the Lord, a relationship that demanded loyalty, commitment and faithfulness.

The Lord is always calling us to draw nearer. He wants more commitment from us, like a lover will say to the beloved: I want us to be closer, I want us to get to know each other better. One way of deepening our relationship with Jesus is to have a place for His Mother in our heart. True devotion to Mary draws us closer to her Son.

The more we become intimate with the Lord, the more he transforms us. John was transformed from being a son of thunder (bad tempered) to an ambassador of love. The more we become intimate with God, the more He reveals Himself to us. He blesses us with divine understanding and knowledge of the mystery of our life and salvation. This is the type of knowledge that Stephen possessed and with which he refuted and defeated his learned opponents.

Through the intercession of St. John, the beloved disciple, may the Lord draw us nearer in love to Himself.

28 DECEMBER

The Holy Innocents, Martyrs

Feast

SPIRITUAL NEGLECT OF CHILDREN

READING TEXTS:
1 John 1:5-2:2; Psalm 124; Matthew 2:13-18

Today, the Holy Mother Church celebrates the feast of the Holy Innocents. These are the innocent children massacred at the order of King Herod in the hope that, by killing every boy born in Bethlehem at the same time as Jesus, he would succeed in killing the new-born King of the Jews.

These babies could not talk; they did nothing wrong, but an evil king chose to terminate their lives out of jealousy for a baby, not minding the agony and sorrows of their mothers.

Crimes against children have continued in different shapes and forms up until today. Today, I want to focus on an aspect not often talked about, that is, spiritual neglect of children. There is so much talk on different forms of neglect today, but little attention is ever paid to the spiritual neglect of children.

This morning, I am preaching on five ways that children can be spiritually neglected.

I.   *Wrong doctrines*

Children are naturally curious and often they uncritically accept whatever we tell them because they trust us so much. If you tell a child that souls in purgatory eat pizza, they will believe and hold onto that.

168

Let me give an example here. A boy of about seven years of age once told me he was a child of the devil. I asked him who told him that. He said that his mum had told him that he was a child of the devil and that's why he is so naughty.

To impress such doctrines on children is wrong.

II.   *When we plant hatred in their innocent hearts*

An example of this is when parents plant enmity in their children against someone, or a family that they have something against; when we damage people's integrity before our children with the intention of making them share our sentiment of bitterness or hatred. Some single parents raise their children telling them how evil their father or mother is, even when this is not the case. The child grows up with a distorted narrative and forms judgements based on the false narratives that are planted in him/her.

Sowing seeds of hatred, revenge or bitterness in a child is a form of spiritual neglect. A child must be taught how to love everyone, even the undeserving. This is what religion is all about.

III.   *When we encourage or permit our children to commit sin or even teach them what is morally destructive*

Some parents encourage their underage children to start dating. If at 12 years of age a girl is encouraged to start dating, it is possible that by the time she is 18 years old, her heart will have already been broken numerous times. How do you expect such a young person to be emotionally stable?

Some parents introduce their children to smoking, drinking, immodest dressing and watching X-rated movies. This is spiritual neglect with negative impacts on their spiritual well-being.

Read Mark 9:42.

IV. When we refuse to plant and nurture the seed of faith in our children

Many parents are commendably concerned to ensure the well-being of their children and they invest heavily in enabling their children's development. However, the most important legacy a child needs is what many parents neglect   faith.

Many parents enroll their children in excellent schools, take them to parks and cinemas and ensure they have exciting holidays. Many parents want to ensure that their children have opportunities to participate in wonderful extra-curricular activities, such as learning musical instruments, dancing and sports etc. but they pay less, or no, attention to their spiritual growth.

Children these days have access to an array of diverse media, including video games, films, cartoons and storybooks. In contrast, many children have never seen or read the book containing the story of their salvation. Those who do have access to a Bible, are often not encouraged to read it. It is not uncommon for a child to be able to recall the Harry Potter stories in great detail and yet know little, or close to nothing, of the stories and messages in the Bible.

To fail in our duty to teach our children the beauty of faith and the joy of a relationship with Jesus is a form of spiritual neglect.

V. When we deny their interest in things of God

In Luke 18:15-16, the disciples of Jesus were trying to prevent children from drawing close to Jesus. Some parents knowingly or unknowingly act like these disciples, becoming obstacles to their children's encounter with the Lord.

I know of a man who stopped his child from serving at Mass, because he was afraid that serving Mass might evoke an interest in the priesthood. Some parents keep their children away from the important sacraments. They neither bring them forward for baptism nor encourage them to receive the Eucharist or even come to Mass. Some parents may prevent their children from going to Church, because they themselves have lost faith and focus.

In one of our schools here, after teaching the children the Lord's prayer and the prayer to our Guardian Angel, a child told me that she loves these prayers but cannot pray them at home because her father had banned them from praying in the house. This is spiritual neglect.

Let us be careful to avoid anything that can impact negatively on the spirituality of our children, anything that can effectively diminish, distort, obscure or impede their spiritual growth. The greatest legacy we can give our children is faith and the greatest investment we can make on behalf of our children is the investment in their spiritual life. Some parents will stand with shame before their judge on their last day because of culpable failure in bringing their children up in the way of the Lord.

St. Thomas Becket, Martyr

READING TEXTS:
1 John 2:3-11; Psalm 95:1-3,5-6; Luke 2:22-35

Today in England and Wales, we celebrate the feast of St Thomas Becket, a martyr and Bishop.

He was born in London and became a close friend of King Henry II. He was only a deacon when he was appointed Chancellor of England. He was ordained as Archbishop of Canterbury in 1162. As an archbishop, he underwent an abrupt conversion of life and began to defend the Church's rights against the king. He had to take refuge in a French monastery for six years, and when he returned to his diocese, four knights, inspired by the king, assassinated him in his cathedral on 29th December 1170. The king had ordered his murder for refusing to give the monarchy power over the church.

He was immediately acknowledged as a martyr and the king later did penance and endowed his shrine. Pope Alexander canonized him in 1173. He is remembered for his courage in the defense of the rights of the Church. Today's feast reminds us to pray for those who suffer unjustly for their faith; those who are being haunted and tortured because they are not ready to compromise their consciences.

This feast reminds us also that every Christian ought to be a potential martyr. Our faith can expose us to

great risks sometimes, but then we must be prepared to
stand always for what we believe, no matter the
consequences. A coward can't be a good Christian.

Today's feast invites us to reflect on those times
when we have tried to force others to act against their
well-formed consciences; have threatened others; have
tried to force people to do our will (even when it is
wrong); have compelled others to obey us in matters that
violate their faith and dignity.

Let us beg for mercy and repent of such.

Books by the same Author

- He Sent Forth His Word, Series 1: Homilies for Sundays, Year A.

- He Sent Forth His Word, Series 2: Homilies for Sundays, Year B.

- He Sent Forth His Word, Series 3: Homilies for Sundays, Year C.

- He Sent Forth His Word, Series 4: Homilies for the Liturgical Seasons of Advent, Christmas, Lent and Easter.

- He Sent Forth His Word, Series 5: Homilies for Feasts and Solemnities.

- He Sent Forth His Word, Series 6: Homilies for Weekdays, Cycle I.

- He Sent Forth His Word, Series 7: Homilies for Weekdays, Cycle II.

- Light to my Path: A Collection of Retreat Talks and Reflections.

- Lord, Teach Us to Pray: Prayers for Various Occasions.

- Praying with the Psalms

- Seven Days Journey with the Lord: A Handbook for a self-facilitated Retreat.

- They Shall Be Called My Children: Short Reflections and Prayers for Children.

- What God has Joined Together: A Handbook for Marriage Preparation Course.

- Whom Shall I Send? A Seven-day Journey with the Lord through His Word.

- When the Spirit Comes Upon You, Series 1: A Nine-day Reflection and Prayers for the Gifts of the Holy Spirit

- When the Spirit Comes Upon You, Series 2: A Twelve-day Reflection and Prayers for the Fruits of the Holy Spirit

- When the Spirit Comes Upon You, Series 3: A Nine-day Reflection and Prayers for the Manifestation of the Holy Spirit.

REFERENCES

The Holy Bible, Revised Standard Version, second Catholic Edition, Ignatian Press, San Francisco, 2006.

New International Version **(NIV)**

Holy Bible, New International Version®, NIV® Copyright ©1973, 1978, 1984, 2011 by Biblica.Inc.

Brown, Raymond Murphy; Fitzmyer Joseph A; Murphy, Roland E, eds (1990).

The New Jerome Biblical Commentary. Eaglewood Cliffs, N.J: Prentice Hall.

David Guzik's Enduring Word Bible Commentary (2018) enduringword.com

Universalis App on Android, version 1.25 (March, 2016) Universalis Publishing Limited

INDEX

Mystery 8,34,49,91,145,164

N

Nathaniel 65,117,135
Nativity of Saint John the Baptist 98
Nativity of the Blessed Virgin Mary 121
Natural Disasters 63
Nazi Party 147
Negation 70
New Testament 33
News 5,21,45,60,95,105,107,125
Non-Believers 2
North Africa 161
Northern France 58

O

Obedience 4,10,20,119,165
Obligations 8
Offences 27
Office 3,23,70,120
Opponents 167
Our Lady, Mother of Africa 63
Our Lady of Fatima 69
Overshadowing 35

P

Palestine 57
Palm Sunday 38,41
Paschal Triduum 41
Paul VI (Pope) 62,67
Pentecost Sunday 81
Persia 134
Physician 131